THE BRONZE AGE
BEGINS

The Ceramics Revolution of Early Minoan I and the New
Forms of Wealth that Transformed Prehistoric Society

Frontispiece. Pithos holding 165 kg with decoration of applied clay moldings. From Early Minoan I, from Aphrodite's Kephali (photograph by Chronis Papanikolopoulos).

THE BRONZE AGE BEGINS

The Ceramics Revolution of Early Minoan I and the New Forms of Wealth that Transformed Prehistoric Society

by

Philip P. Betancourt

Published by
INSTAP Academic Press
Philadelphia, PA
2008

Design and Production
INSTAP Academic Press

Printing
CRWGraphics, Pennsauken, New Jersey

Binding
McCormick's Bindery, Inc., Pennsauken, New Jersey

Library of Congress Cataloging-in-Publication Data

Betancourt, Philip P., 1936–
 The Bronze Age begins : the ceramics revolution of early Minoan I and the new forms of
wealth that transformed prehistoric society / by Philip P. Betancourt.
        p. cm.
 Includes bibliographical references and index.
  ISBN 978-1-931534-52-9 (pbk.)
 1. Pottery, Minoan—Greece—Crete. 2. Ceramics—Greece—Crete—History. 3. Crete
(Greece)—Antiquities. 4. Bronze age—Greece—Crete. 5. Wealth—Social aspects—
Greece—Crete—History—To 1500. 6. Social change—Greece—Crete—History—To 1500.
7. Crete (Greece)—Social conditions. 8. Crete (Greece)—Economic conditions. I. Title.
  DF221.C8B54 2008
  939'.1801—dc22

                                                                        2009006204

The transition from the Neolithic to the Minoan Bronze Age is defined in terms of radical changes in pottery fashions.

Sinclair Hood, *The Minoans*
1971

Table of Contents

List of Figures

Preface

This is a book about economic and social changes and how they occur. Its focus is the opening phase of the Minoan "civilization" on the island of Crete, which is a useful venue for examining such cultural transformations, because we have a considerable amount of evidence for this early phase in human history. The conclusion is that new developments in ceramics that reached Crete at the end of the Neolithic period acted as the final piece in a set of complex factors that were already converging to create the economic, technological, social, and religious advancements we call the Early Bronze Age. The arguments are set out in two parts, a detailed explanation of the ceramics we call Early Minoan I and the differences that set it apart from its predecessors, and an explanation of how these new and highly superior containers changed the storage, transport, and accumulation of a new form of wealth consisting primarily of agricultural and animal products. The increased stability and security provided by an improved ability to store food from one year to the next would have a profound effect on the society.

The book is dedicated to the many graduate students who undertook pottery projects in my courses at Temple University's Tyler School of Art suburban campus. Between 1970 when I began teaching at the university and 2008 when the campus moved into its new building in Philadelphia, I offered a seminar where graduate students had an opportunity to experiment with ancient technology. In addition to making faience, building warp-weighted looms, working on various metals techniques, and other possibilities, the students could undertake various ceramics projects including building a wood-burning kiln. The kilns were especially successful vehicles for understanding more about ancient pyrotechnology, and students learned the subtle differences in construction design that can affect the resulting effectiveness of the firing. Some of the projects resulted in publications (Betancourt et al. 1979; Betancourt, Berkowitz, and Zaslow 1990; Gosser and Sapareto 1984), while others were simply presented as seminar papers. All of the projects led to a better appreciation of ancient technology by the instructor as well as the students.

Acknowledgments

Many people deserve thanks for the information presented here. Much of the research was conducted in connection with excavations supported by Temple University and the Institute for Aegean Prehistory, both located in Philadelphia, Pennsylvania. I am grateful to my colleagues Peter Warren and Robert Koehl for reading early versions of this book and offering several useful suggestions. Some of the most helpful ideas were developed in connection with the study of Hagia Photia Siteias, in collaboration with my good friend Costis Davaras, and Aphrodite's Kephali, for which thanks are expressed to Theodore Eliopoulos and Stavroula Apostolakou for permission to publish this site and its pottery. I am grateful to Yannis Tzedakis and Maria Vlasaki for the images and information about vases from West Crete.

The illustrations come from sources that are cited in the captions. Drawings and photographs without credits are by the author.

Abbreviations

Abbreviations of journals not listed here follow the conventions used by the *American Journal of Archaeology* 111.1 (2007), pp. 14–34.

AK	Aphrodite's Kephali
C	Celcius
Chania	Chania, Archaeological Museum
ca.	approximately
cm	centimeter
dia.	diameter
EC	Early Cycladic
EM	Early Minoan
FN	Final Neolithic
gr	gram(s)
HCH	Hagios Charalambos Cave
HM	Herakleion, Archaeological Museum
HNM	Hagios Nikolaos, Archaeological Museum
ht.	height
INSTAP-SCEC	INSTAP Study Center for East Crete, Pacheia Ammos, Crete
km	kilometers
KrChron	*Kritika Chronika*
LM	Late Minoan
m	meters
mm	millimeters
MM	Middle Minoan
PAR	Pacheia Ammos Rock Shelter

pers. comm.   personal communication
PS   Pseira
SEM   Scanning Electron Microscopy

Part I

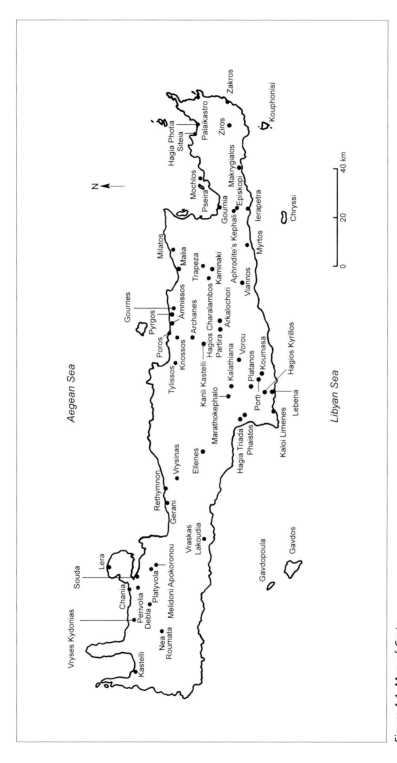

Figure 1.1. Map of Crete.

1

Introduction

In the continent that would later be named Europe, the set of complex urban experiences we term "civilization" began on the island of Crete (Fig. 1.1). The earliest phase developed as a long and gradual process with small changes in economics, agriculture, social advancement, technology, and many other areas of human achievement. Archaeology is the most important tool for learning about this island and the nearby lands that fronted on the Aegean Sea during this early period at the close of the fourth and the beginning of the third millennium B.C. Pottery was an essential commodity in these cultures, and its study provides us with valuable information on the history of the people who made and used it.

Crete played a dominant role in the early history of the Aegean. The Minoan culture of this large island developed the first writing system in the region, and its brilliant palatial society of the second millennium B.C. expanded enough to be remembered in mythology long before archaeologists began to study it seriously. The Early Bronze Age, in the previous millennium, was the earliest stage of the society.

In his landmark 1972 book on this period called *The Emergence of Civilisation*, Colin Renfrew made a strong case for an intensification of complexity during the second stage of the Aegean Early Bronze Age. More recent work has shown that many of his ideas were correct (for critical discussion of this work, see Barrett and Halstead, eds., 2004). The international spirit of the Early Bronze II period was a time of unprecedented advances in trade, technology, economic development, and social actions throughout the Aegean region, with metals playing a major role in the new situation.

From Crete, Early Bronze II foreign trade reached as far as the eastern shores of the Mediterranean (Colburn 2008). The present study looks at the immediately preceding period on the large island at the south of the Aegean Sea. The conclusions are based on an especially large amount of fresh evidence, most of it excavated in the last 20 years. These new pieces of information help fill in some of the earlier stages that led up to that rapid development in Early Bronze II, and they suggest that many of the advances of Early Minoan II need to be pushed back to the preceding period.

The island of Crete has always presented special problems. It played an important role in the later development of Aegean society, but its earliest phases remain obscure. Until recently the first stage of the Bronze Age, called Early Minoan I in Crete, has been characterized primarily from its architecture and its pottery rather than from a full range of artifacts. It has long been recognized that the beginning of the Minoan period included both local development and stimuli from overseas (Hood 1971, 29; 1990a; 1990b). The arrival of new tomb types at about this time or slightly earlier, including the monumental vaulted tholos tombs of south-central Crete (Xanthoudides 1924; Branigan 1970b), provides dramatic evidence of new concepts emerging, and surely new groups of people were arriving, but we are still unsure about exactly from where some of these foreign concepts came or how they interacted with local ideas. In many cases, we cannot be sure if an innovation that looks new arrived from abroad or actually developed slowly in Crete itself from the little-known Neolithic experiences.

Summary of the Chronology

Early Minoan I is defined by its pottery, some of which is very different from the ceramics of the preceding Final Neolithic period. The most dramatic style of the new age is a class made of pale-firing clay that was decorated with very bold linear designs in red slip. The pottery appears suddenly in Crete, with no obvious antecedents. An origin in the Chalcolithic of Israel and Palestine has been proposed because red-painted ceramics occurs there as well (Weinberg 1965, 307; Koehl 2008), but the suggestion has problems because few of the other aspects of this particular eastern culture have any parallels in Crete. The truth is that one can find a number of aspects of Early Minoan I that recall similar items from elsewhere, but no close correspondence has been found in the archaeological record as a whole to establish an original site for even a specific Minoan technology like the making of a particular class of ceramics, much less for the main aspects of Minoan society as a whole. We are left with the supposition that the technology for this revolutionary type of Minoan pottery, which turned out superior products in hardness and density and allowed vases over a meter high to be successfully fired, was so subtly changed when it arrived in Crete that we can no longer identify its exact origins.

Crete had a large Bronze Age population (Figs. 1.1–1.5). Many Early Minoan I deposits are known, and some of them contain large assemblages of pottery. Early Minoan I is stratified above Final Neolithic at Kephala Petras (Papadatos 2006), an open-air settlement in eastern Crete. The large cemetery at Hagia Photia is also mostly from this period (Davaras and Betancourt 2004). A deep well with much EM I pottery comes from Knossos (Hood 1990a; Wilson 2007). Poros-Katsambas, the port of Knossos, has a good assemblage of sherds (Dimopoulou-Rethemiotaki, Wilson, and Day 2007; Wilson, Day, and Dimopoulou-Rethemiotaki 2008). Abundant material comes from caves at Pyrgos (Xanthoudides 1918a), Kyparissi (Alexiou 1951), and several places in West Crete (Tzedakis 1984). In the Mesara, good deposits come from Phaistos and Hagia Triada (Todaro 2001), from the lower level in Lebena Tomb II (Alexiou and Warren 2004), and from Koutsokera (Xanthoudides 1924, pl. 40a). A

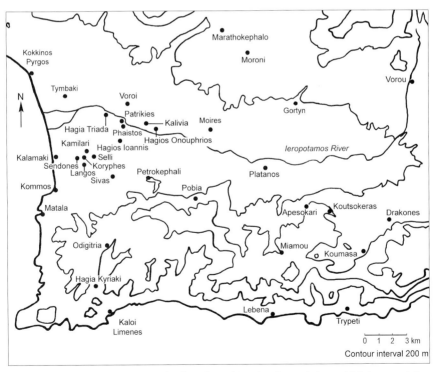

Figure 1.2. Map of the Mesara. The location of Hagios Onouphrios, which is uncertain, follows the map of Xanthoudides (1924).

tholos at Krasi has many vases (Marinatos 1929b). Debla is an important site in West Crete (Warren and Tzedhakis 1974). Other deposits exist as well. In addition to earlier groups of objects, the recent publications of

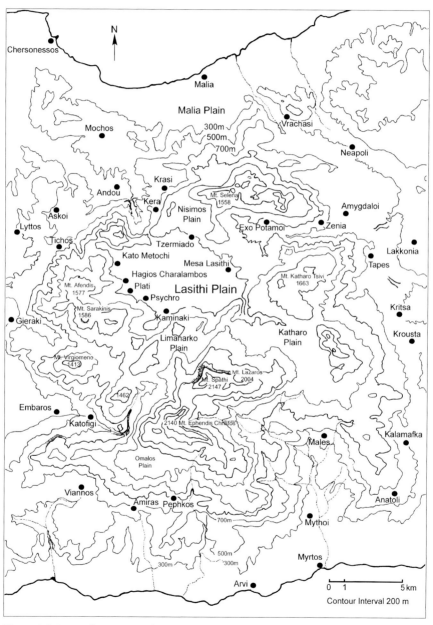

Figure 1.3. Map of East-Central Crete.

large numbers of EM I vases from Hagia Photia and Lebena and the recent excavation of Aphrodite's Kephali (Betancourt 2008) contribute especially important information.

In relative terms, Early Minoan I begins at the time of the Grotta-Pelos Group in the Cyclades (Warren and Hankey 1989, 21–23, with earlier bibliography). Cycladic bottles in the Pelos Style (also called Pelos Ware) occur in several contexts in Crete (see discussion in Ch. 5). For the end of the period, the latest EM I deposit is the assemblage from the Hagia Photia cemetery where the earliest examples of Fine Gray pottery have already appeared alongside vases of pure EM I type. The Fine Gray vases (Fig. 1.6) are primarily from the next period (compare the EM IIA vase published by Davaras 2003, 164, fig. 75a), but their presence here provides a cautionary note that pottery fashions did not all change at once. This part of the period is contemporary with the Kampos Group in the Cyclades. The Kampos Group, the cultural assemblage in the Aegean Islands that follows the Grotta-Pelos Group and can be placed at the transition between EC I and EC II, has more to do with the earlier phase than the later one (Rambach 2000, 48–57; see also Renfrew 1972, 527–528; 1984; Doumas 1977; Weinberg 1976, 143; MacGillivray 1984; Warren 1984; Wilson and Eliot 1984; Coleman 1985; Barber 1987, 27; Branigan 1988b, 239, 244; Warren and Hankey 1989, 22–23, 34; Cosmopoulos 1991, 118; Manning 1995, 45–48; Karantzali 1996, 59; Broodbank 2000, fig. 98 and passim). Many Kampos Group vases circulated in Crete, and a selection is discussed in Chapter 5 in this study.

The exact chronological date for the beginning of EM I is uncertain. The earliest appearance of the pottery classes that define it have been placed within ca. 3600/3500–3000/2900 B.C. by Peter Warren and Vronwy Hankey (1989, 169), in 3200 B.C. by Saul Weinberg (1965, 313), in ca. 3100–3000 B.C. by Sturt Manning (1995, 168–170), and in 2600 B.C. by Nicolas Platon (1974, 118). Manning's use of calibrated radiocarbon dates for the Anatolian cultures that appear to be contemporary suggests that his date is probably to be preferred, but one cannot be certain.

The Economy

The general parameters of the Neolithic and Final Neolithic cultures in Crete are fairly well known (Vagnetti 1996; Vagnetti and Belli 1978). The people were farmers and herders who tilled the land and raised grains, vegetables, and a few fruit trees. Most of the people lived in small villages and walked out to their fields, but a few larger towns existed as well, and Knossos was already a modest city. The island had had a small population

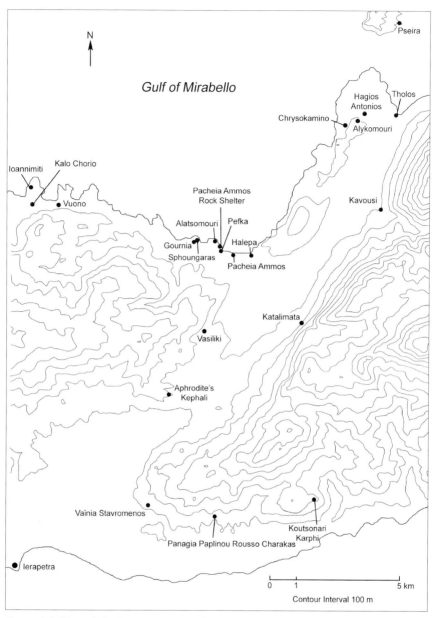

Figure 1.4. Map of the Ierapetra Peninsula.

for millennia, but new residents were still arriving, and the island was still empty enough to absorb newcomers. Seafaring in some type of boat or ship was known, as is shown by the many Final Neolithic sites placed on excellent harbors, but most of the sea traffic was probably with the nearby

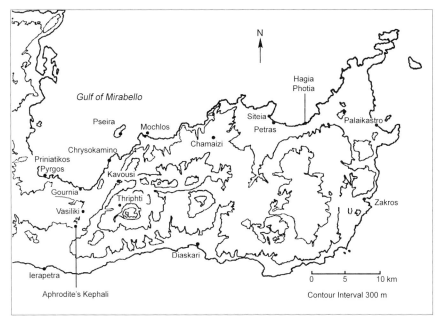

Figure 1.5. Map of East Crete.

and familiar places along the coast. This general domestic economy was not very different from what existed in many other places across a broad geographic region from southeast Europe to Anatolia where people raised the same domestic animals (sheep, goats, pigs, and a few cattle), made similar chipped and ground stone tools, and raised the same crops, especially barley, wheat, oats, and legumes (Broodbank and Strasser 1991; van Andel and Runnels 1995). When the making of pottery began, most of these agriculturalists made dark, burnished pottery that was fired in enclosed spaces in proximity with a fire that had to burn for many hours to turn the vases into low-fired ceramics. By the end of the Neolithic many regions had developed much more sophisticated pottery (for example, the beautifully decorated wares of Sesklo and Dimeni in northern Greece), but such advanced technology had not yet reached Crete. This situation is the background for what would happen in EM I.

The new vessels that were made in EM I had a profound effect on the domestic economy of Crete. They were harder, denser, and more durable than the Final Neolithic ones. They were quickly adopted as storage and shipping containers for a variety of products, many of which belong to what has been called the secondary products revolution (Sherratt 1981; 1983). Secondary agricultural and pastoral products include cheese, yogurt, woolen cloth, olive oil, wine, and other commodities that are made by processing the animal products and harvested crops that were raised by early agriculturalists. These items have several advantages over the primary ones. The secondary animal products can be shipped more easily than live creatures, and (unlike meat and leather) the livestock does not have to be killed, so the flocks and herds are a sustainable resource that continues to produce valuable commodities for food, clothing, and exchange. The agricultural goods include a long list of things that can be stored and shipped: wine and vinegar produced from grapes can be consumed, and they can also be used as preservatives for fruits and vegetables. Other liquids, like brine and honey, are also useful to retard spoilage of more perishable products. The improvements in EM I pottery facilitated the storage and shipment of many commodities, particularly essential food products, with far-reaching consequences.

Nomenclature

The nomenclature used for Early Minoan pottery in this publication includes several specific terms. A class is any group of vases that share characteristics of any type. The word fabric is used for the fired clay of a ceramic object, defined by its composition, structure, color, and other characteristics. A fabric group consists of two or more similar-appearing fabrics whose individual members can only be distinguished through microscopic analysis using petrographic thin sections, although the group as a whole can be recognized by eye. A specific fabric (rather than a fabric group) must have its definition described on the basis of ceramic petrography, because the base clay must be identified in addition to the larger inclusions. A style is a group of vases sharing characteristics of surface treatment and decoration. Because styles are defined in this way and not on the basis of fabric, a style can be made in more than one fabric, or a fabric

Figure 1.6. Fine Gray Style pyxis from Hagia Photia Siteias, Tomb 211, HNM 4207 (photograph by Chronis Papanikolopoulos). Ht. 11 cm.

can be used for more than one style. The specifically named styles mostly follow the suggestions for wares as characterized by Branigan (1970a) and Betancourt (1985).

In the past, the term ware has been used in several different ways. It has been defined on the basis of style (i.e., Pyrgos Ware and Hagios Onouphrios Ware: Betancourt 1985), by the texture (i.e., coarse ware or fine ware), or even based on the use (i.e., cooking ware). Because in this study the word style is used for specific classes of decoration, the term ware is reserved for a class of pottery where both a specific style and a specific fabric or fabric group are known, such as for the red-painted pottery in the Hagios Onouphrios Style that was made in the South Coast Fabric Group, which would be called South Coast Hagios Onouphrios Ware (for example, a fragment from Knossos described by Wilson and Day 1994, 69).

Descriptions of coarse and fine textures for fabrics are based on the size of the inclusions. Fine-textured fabrics have inclusions that are mostly less than 1 mm in size. Medium-textured fabrics have inclusions that are mostly from 1 mm to 5 mm. Coarse-textured fabrics have many included fragments greater than 5 mm in size.

2

The Change in Ceramic Technology in EM I

The changes in pottery that establish the interface between what we call the Stone Age and the Bronze Age in Crete involved the adoption of a whole new technology—much more than just different vase shapes or new decorations. New practices involved fresh ideas in the selection of raw materials, the clay preparation, the shapes that were manufactured, the treatment of the surfaces, the ornament, and the way to fire the vessels. In other words, EM I brought transformative changes leading to entirely new methods of making vases out of clay.

The EM I pottery and its new technology can only be understood by comparing it with the manufacturing practices that preceded it. The Neolithic technology was not completely abandoned at the beginning of the Early Bronze Age. Many parts of it continued, and they affected the products that were made in the new historical period.

Final Neolithic Ceramic Technology

The Final Neolithic pottery of Crete was all made by hand from fabric recipes that included large amounts of stone fragments, often with additional pieces of plant materials to make the vases coarser and more porous. A detail of a Minoan vase made with this technology is shown in Figure 2.1. The surface has numerous pits from the voids caused by plant stems and other organic materials that burned away during the firing, and the large pieces of white stone included in the clay are also visible. These

Figure 2.1. Detail of a coarse, dark vessel using the Final Neolithic technology, from a rock shelter at Pacheia Ammos, PAR 46. The voids (black areas) showing on the surface are mostly caused by organic matter that burned away during the firing, leaving a highly porous fabric (photograph by the author, by courtesy of Stavroula Apostolakou and Thomas Brogan). Size of field ca. 2.2 cm.

inclusions, called temper, did not shrink like the clay did when it was dried and fired, so they caused less change in the volume (which reduced cracking and breaking), and they also created a porous clay body so that water vapor and other gases could escape during firing instead of causing the vase to break when it was heated. The materials used as temper varied between production centers, and they included crushed pieces of white carbonate (calcite or marble), various other stones that were probably locally available to the potters, and plant materials, especially the short-chopped pieces of grain stalks left over after threshing removed the grain (called chaff).

In the vase shown in Figure 2.1, the temper consists of both calcite (which is calcium carbonate [$CaCO_3$]) and organic matter. These materials will have changed the characteristics of the vase in various ways. In addition to decreasing the amount of shrinkage and allowing gases to escape during firing, the rock fragments also block and change the direction of tiny voids, preventing them from becoming larger. The organic materials decrease the breakage during drying by increasing the rate of evaporation (London 1981, 193–194). The calcite can lower the temperature at which vitrification begins (Tite and Maniatis 1975; Maniatis and Tite 1978, 484–485), which would have been useful for low-fired ceramics. On the other hand, not all of the characteristics created by these two tempering materials are beneficial. At ca. 650–850°C, the calcite decomposes and releases carbon dioxide that can cause breakage. The addition of the organic material significantly lowers the hardness of the final product, making it more fragile, because it burns away and leaves voids (London 1981, 192). This porosity would also cause the vases to leak as water or other liquids moved slowly through the fabric.

The porosity of the Cretan Final Neolithic vases was countered by the process called burnishing. After the vase was built by the potter but before it was completely dry, the surface was compressed by rubbing it with a smooth tool like a polished bone or a smooth pebble. Both the interiors and the exteriors of open containers like bowls were burnished, but only the outside of closed vessels could be reached after they were almost dry. The burnishing smoothed the microscopic clay platelets and left them aligned with the surface, and it also compressed the clay and closed open pores, making the vessels more water-tight.

Cretan Final Neolithic pottery was often dark brown, gray, or black in color. Surfaces were often variegated, and the interior core of the fabric was usually solid gray or black, characteristics that result from firing the pottery in an enclosed environment like a hearth or a hole in the ground with a fire built over it (pit-firing). High enough temperatures can easily be achieved on a windy day by simply stacking the fuel around the vessels to be fired and allowing the fire to burn for an extended period, and a temperature as high as 962°C has been recorded with this type of firing (Shepard 1956, 83). Because the vases are covered by the ashes and carbon and fuel, this method creates dark pottery. The dark color is mainly caused by iron, a common constituent of clays that is present in two ways, as iron oxides and as part of the crystal lattice of many minerals. When they are heated, iron oxides change easily between red ferric oxide (Fe_2O_3) and black ferrous oxide (FeO) depending on whether carbon dioxide or carbon monoxide is present (Hess and Perlman 1974). If water vapor is also in contact with the material, magnetite, another black iron oxide, and other oxides, including very black species like hercynite, can form as well (Noll 1978, 503). In a covered fire, a pit, or a hearth, the incomplete combustion of the fuel forms carbon monoxide (called a reducing atmosphere because little air can get to the fire), and this situation forms the black iron oxides. Usually at least a little oxygen is present in sufficient amounts to form some carbon dioxide (otherwise the fire would go out), making the vases partly dark brown or reddish brown.

Progressive changes take place in ceramics as the vases are fired (summaries of the most important stages are given by Jones 1986, 751; Evely 2000, 299; and Lawrence 1972, 55–56). Absorbed water is lost as steam at about 100–200°C. Dehydroxylation begins at 400°C and continues to about 800°C, as hydroxides change to oxides with additional loss of water vapor. At about 450°C the crystal lattice of the clay begins to collapse with substantial shrinkage of the volume. Many of the hydroxides are iron minerals, so the release of iron oxides can substantially change the color of the resulting vessels in comparison with the original clay. Sintering, the melting and bonding together of the outer surfaces of the tiny iron oxide particles, begins at about 600°C (Shepard 1956, 174–175), and the slight initial melting of the clay fabric begins at about this temperature as well. The firing has to reach above 600°C for the vessels to be hard enough to be useful, but this temperature is not difficult to achieve, and pottery fired to 625°C in a simple fire has been documented (Shephard 1956, 83). Although the vitrification process begins at this point, the vases will be harder, denser, and more solid with higher temperatures and increased melting of the fabric at the microscopic level. At ca. 650–850°C, calcium carbonate decomposes (Jones 1986, 754). The Final Neolithic vases that were tempered with calcite or marble could not be allowed to reach this temperature, because when the calcareous inclusions decompose they suddenly release carbon dioxide that may break the vessels. Calcium silicates form at 850–1050°C. Vitrification advances after 1050°C.

All of these stages in firing pottery are averages and approximations, because the processes take place at different temperatures based on many factors including variations in grain size, composition, presence or absence of other constituents, and type of kiln atmosphere. A lower temperature maintained for a longer period can equal the results of a higher temperature kept for a shorter time (Heimann 1982, 89). The presence or absence of fluxing agents also affects the vitrification. In an oxidizing atmosphere, vitrification occurs at a higher temperature than when oxygen is absent. Because an oxygen-depleted (reducing) atmosphere lowers the vitrification point (Maniatis and Tite 1975; Maniatis, Simopoulos, and Kostikas 1983), the blocking of oxygen in the covered and enclosed Final Neolithic pits and hearths was an important aspect of the technology that produced useful pottery with lower temperatures. The dark colors were a natural result of the reducing atmosphere during firing.

The New Technology

The Hagios Onouphrios Style jug in Figure 2.2 illustrates one of the vases made with the new Early Minoan I technology. It was found in a tomb in south-central Crete where it was deposited as an offering to the deceased. The vase is a jug with a raised spout and a rounded base. It was manufactured from pale-firing clay, covered with an overall coat of almost white slip, and then decorated with dark red linear designs before being fired in a well-constructed kiln that finished the vase successfully. Its presence indicates that a new technology had arrived in Crete, and it differs from its Neolithic predecessors both in its outer appearance and in its hardness and durability. A detail of the surface (Fig. 2.3) illustrates the careful painting on a pale colored overall slip that covers the exterior of the vase.

Figure 2.2. EM I jug from Hagios Onouphrios, a burial site near Phaistos in southern Crete, HM 5. Ht. 21.5 cm.

Some important aspects of the changes in ceramics that help us define Early Minoan I can be illustrated by the pottery excavated from the EM I site of Aphrodite's Kephali, a fortified watchtower in the Isthmus of Ierapetra (Betancourt 2008). The evidence from this small single-period site shows that the adoption of the new ceramic technology occurred over a considerable length of time. The Cretan workshops responded different-ly to the new ideas, and some of them adopted only part of the new tech-nology. In the ceramics from this site, after sherds were joined together and mended, the corpus of pottery consisted of 594 fragments and vases. The pottery was very fragmentary, and no complete vessels could be assembled, although small and large sections of some examples were put together from

Figure 2.3. Detail of the surface of the Hagios Onouphrios Style name-vase, HM 5.

the scattered pieces. Dividing these fragments by technological class led to some interesting statistics, presented graphically in Figure 2.4. These statistics demonstrated that not all of the pottery was made with the same manufacturing system:

1. A total of 9.8% of the fragments consisted of sherds using the FN technology in its entirety. Clay was tempered with a variety of coarse materials, including white angular carbonate (calcite or marble), phyllite, other stones, and organic material, sometimes with more than one aplastic substance in the same fabric. Vessels were manufactured with thick walls. They were fired in a pit or hearth, sometimes in contact with the fuel, to produce variegated colors that were usually very dark. Most of these sherds were black or dark gray, and all of them were heavily burnished to create a lustrous, smooth surface.

2. A total of 28% of the fragments were made of clay that was prepared in the same way as in the FN, with coarse temper consisting of angular white carbonate fragments. The walls of the vessels were thick, but the surfaces were just wiped instead of burnished. These vases were fired in a kiln in an oxidizing atmosphere, which made the surfaces red to brown. In other words, the vases combined the clay preparation and part of the manufacturing technology from the Final Neolithic period with a new surface treatment and firing system.

3. A total of 4% of the sherds used fine-textured marl clays to create a fine, even fabric without any coarse temper. The vases were manufactured with thin walls, but they were heavily burnished before being fired in a pit or hearth. The final products, which were low fired and brown to dark gray, used the older system for surface finishing and firing technology but the new system of clay choice, clay preparation, and vessel manufacture.

4. A total of 57% of the pottery used the new technology in its entirety. The fabrics were made with a high percentage of fine-grained marl clays, the vases were never tempered with carbonate fragments, surfaces were wiped or covered with slip, and the firing was accomplished in a kiln. These sherds were always pale colored, and many were decorated with a red-firing slip that either covered the vessel completely or was used for linear ornament.

These statistics illustrate the transitional nature of EM I ceramic technology. The pottery found at this site came from several different sources. Some of the active workshops of this period adopted the new technology, others used just part of it, and a few potters continued to make the same type of vessels that had been traditional for many generations. At Aphrodite's Kephali, the vases made entirely with the older technology may have been used primarily (or exclusively?) as cooking vessels.

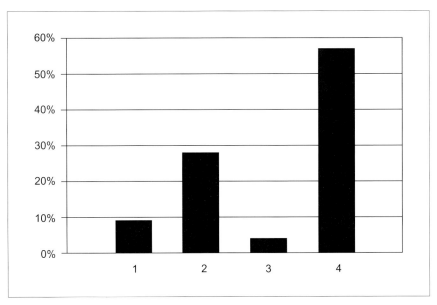

Figure 2.4. Graph showing the relative percentages of different technologies identified in the sherds from Aphrodite's Kephali: 1. sherds using all FN technology; 2. sherds with FN clay recipe but not burnished and fired in a kiln; 3. sherds with EM I clay recipe and shape but burnished and fired dark; 4. sherds using all EM I technology.

As these sherds demonstrate, the technology that was introduced into Crete at the beginning of the Early Bronze Age involved new practices at all stages in the production of pottery from clay selection to firing of the finished products. Recipes for the fabric were changed, clays were prepared in fresh ways, new shapes were manufactured, surfaces were treated differently, and a previously unknown pyrotechnology was employed to fire the vases.

In the new way of manufacturing ceramics, the first step, as always, was the digging of the clay and its preparation. Modern potters in Crete who use traditional methods have almost always mixed their fabrics by blending a pale-colored marl clay with a red terra rossa sediment, using different proportions of the two ingredients to adjust for the character of individual clay deposits and to create a stiffer or more plastic clay to accommodate the desired recipe for what they were making (Voyatzoglou 1972, 19; 1984, 133; Provatakis 2007, 47). These two ingredients both contain clay minerals, but most of the Cretan marls are too plastic and sticky to make good pottery, and the terra rossa is not plastic enough if used by itself. The geology of the clay deposits has not changed since the Bronze Age, so it is not surprising that evidence for mixing can be noted with the microscopic examination of petrographic thin sections of Minoan vases. These traces of ancient mixed clays are what one would expect based on the nature of the available materials on this isolated island.

The Early Bronze Age potters must have mixed their clays as both their predecessors and their descendants did, but if they were adopting the entire EM I technology, they made two changes in clay preparation. First, they used more Neogene marl clay to create a finer texture and a more calcareous composition than what had been common in the Cretan Neolithic. This change was an innovation in Crete, but it had already been used for millennia in parts of the Near East (Goren and Gopher 1995, 24). Second, when they were making small shapes, the EM I potters left out the large fragments of stone and the organic matter that had been added formerly. Coarse fabrics were not necessary for vases that would be fired in the new kilns. In a kiln chamber, the air circulates quickly, and if the kiln is designed properly and vases are placed in it in the right way, a uniform temperature will exist all around each vase, and the temperature can be raised slowly and evenly, preventing breakage. The success of the EM I results indicates that the potters were well aware of how to design their kilns and how to load and fire them properly.

The increased use of the Neogene marl clays would have also affected the vases during the firing, because this material contains more calcium carbonate than the terra rossa. Calcium carbonate is one of the materials that acts as a flux to help lower the point at which vitrification begins

(Tite and Maniatis 1975; Maniatis and Tite 1978, 484–485; Jones 1986, 757, table 9.5). As the temperature is raised, the calcium carbonate breaks down, forming CaO. The calcium begins to form calcium silicates at temperatures above 700°C. Studies have shown that higher calcareous contents (more than 5% remaining even after firing) also affect the clay above 850°C by creating a cellular vitrification stage that is maintained for ca. 200 degrees (Maniatis and Tite 1978, 485; Maniatis, Simopoulos, and Kostikas 1981; 1983). The advantage of the small-sized calcium carbonate in the marl clays over the larger fragments that were added by the potters in the calcite-tempered FN recipes concerns the decomposition of the carbonate that occurs at ca. 650–850°C. This decomposition releases carbon dioxide that may cause the vessel to break, but the chemical change is a much more severe problem with large fragments than with tiny ones.

Calcareous clays also retard the formation of iron oxides (Jones 1986, 759), so clay bodies with greater marl contents will be pale, allowing a good contrast for decoration using iron-rich slips that will fire dark red under oxidizing conditions. The situation encourages the development of ornament. Fine decoration makes the vases more attractive, but it has other purposes as well. An important benefit of the ease in decorating the new vessels will have been the ability to make a product instantly recognizable by its container. The ability to remember what is in a particular vase is valuable for marketing, and it is also helpful for normal use within a household that needs to occasionally retrieve a specific product from a storeroom filled with pots.

Changes were also made in vessel manufacture. The new shapes could be larger and thinner-walled because they were more durable. With denser and more vitrified fabrics, surfaces no longer needed to be burnished. New shapes were now designed for specific purposes, like jugs with spouts for pouring, small rounded pyxides with lids for small-scale storage, and pithoi of large size for long-term maintenance of commodities needed in bulk amounts.

One of the most important of these new changes, of course, was the introduction of the new type of potter's kiln. The basic principle was that the fire was built in a separate chamber from where the vases were placed. A connection between the two parts of the kiln allowed the heat to rise and flow across and between the vases, gradually building up the temperature as the walls, floor, and ceiling of the kiln absorbed heat. Kilns had been used for a long period in some other parts of the prehistoric Aegean, like the Sesklo and Dimeni cultures of northern Greece (Otto 1985), but they only arrived in Crete at the beginning of EM I. These kilns had several advantages over the earlier Cretan Neolithic firing systems in which the vases were in contact with the fuel or were buried in a pit below the fire.

First, they could reach higher temperatures than were possible previously, so the final products could be harder and denser. Second, they could produce more even temperature ranges within the kiln chamber during the process, with the result that vessels could be heated uniformly instead of having part of the vase hotter than the other side. The even temperatures reduced the uneven shrinkage that occurred when one part of a vase became hotter than another part, so the vases did not have to be so coarse textured to keep them from breaking. The even temperatures also meant that larger vases could be fired. Vessels as large as the pithoi of EM I, which could hold up to 165 liters, could never be fired in a hearth or pit because one side of the vases would get hotter than the other side more quickly, and the vase would break during firing.

In addition, with the new kilns the potters could now control the atmosphere during firing. This aspect of the technology would become one of the main defining features of Minoan pottery in later times (Noll, Holm, and Born 1971–1974), and it has been used to distinguish between Minoan and Cycladic technology (Marthari 1990, 452). Colors in Minoan pottery are mostly caused by the iron in the clay. If vases are fired without oxygen present, the clay turns black, and if oxygen is present, the clay turns red to reddish yellow to pink (for modern experiments with the technology, see Betancourt et al. 1979, 14–16; Lawrence 1972, 170; Alexander 1978). The simple chemical changes that determine red to brown to black colors in ceramics are well understood today from both experimentation and analysis (Hess and Perlman 1974), but they can also be easily observed informally and used to deliberately control the color of the finished product. If the potter keeps the outer door to the firebox open and allows plenty of air to pass into the kiln, the vases become red to reddish yellow to pink. If the firebox door is closed, the fuel will burn up all the oxygen, and the vases will begin to turn dark.

Minoan kilns are only known from later than the beginning of Early Minoan I, but even if the details of the earliest ones were different, the principles have to have been similar. They consisted of a separate chamber for the fire (the firebox), a space for the vases, and a chimney to pull the heat from the fire up to where the pottery was stacked and then out at the top of the kiln. The natural draft created by the fire pulled the heat across the vases by taking advantage of the fact that hot air rises because it is lighter than cold air. Because no glazes that melt were used, the vessels could touch one another during firing.

The reconstruction shown in Figure 2.5 illustrates how a Minoan kiln dating to a later period worked. The kiln, from LM IA Kommos, uses all the principles that would have been present in the earlier constructions as well. This class is called a crossdraft channel kiln because the heat from the firebox is pulled across the vases that are placed in a separate space near the firebox but at a slightly higher level. A chimney creates a strong draft that pulls the heat through a series of channels and conducts it across and between the vases stacked above the channels. Kilns would have been constructed mostly of clay and stones. Their details and shapes could have varied, but they would all have required a firebox with a door to allow the insertion of fuel over a period of many hours, a separate but connected kiln chamber at a higher level for the vases, and a chimney to assist with the draft.

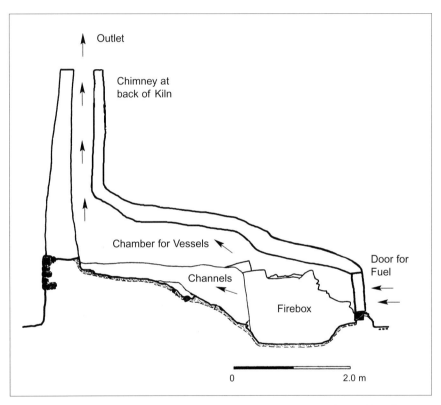

Figure 2.5. Theoretical reconstruction of the superstructure over the channel kiln from Kommos, Crete, LM IA.

3

The Clays and the
Fired Fabrics

The fabric is the clay body after firing, with its characteristics derived from its original constituents plus the long history of its preparation and modification by the potters in the process of manufacturing the ceramics. Many different fabrics can be identified from EM I deposits. Some of them seem to have been strictly local, while others were distributed regionally, and a few were disbursed throughout many parts of Crete. The different fabrics can be distinguished by their inclusions as well as by coarseness, color, texture, and other traits.

The Evidence from Traditional Potters in Crete

Because Cretan geology determines the nature of the island's clays, and their properties have not changed since the Bronze Age, a study of the ways that traditional potters have used those clays can contribute useful knowledge for ancient pottery making, especially on the preparation and treatment of the raw materials. Pottery making was a major profession in Crete until modern times, and potters provided containers of various types to a population that was mostly agrarian. Ceramic vessels were used for cooking, for storage, for keeping water cool, and for many other purposes. The traditional workshops turned out a steady stream of products, all of which used the local Cretan clays. The best known centers were located at

Margaritis (Hampe and Winter 1962, 33–35; Vallianos and Padouva 1986; Leontidis 1996), Kendri (Blitzer 1984; Day 2004, 114–115), and Thrapsano (Xanthoudides 1927; Hampe and Winter 1962, 4–11, 16–32, 35–40; Voyatzoglou 1972; 1974; 1984; Vallianos and Padouva 1986; Day 2004, 111–114), but pottery establishments were situated throughout the island (Psaropoulou 1996, 109; Sklavenitis 1996; Day 2004). In contrast with the other pottery centers, which used permanent quarters, the potters from Thrapsano were itinerant craftsmen who traveled out from their home village and set up small workshops that used local clay sources to serve the immediate vicinity near their temporary locations. The main product of the Thrapsaniote potters was the large jar called the pithari.

Although finished pottery was regularly imported into Crete from several other places, the traditional potters do not seem to have used any clays that were not native to the island until after the middle of the 20th century. Instead, they exploited the hundreds of local sources of raw materials that occur naturally in Crete itself. Most of these clays come from two very different geological environments.

The first class of clays is created principally from the dissolution of local carbonate rocks (limestone and dolomite). When the rocks are exposed to the elements, the carbonate component is dissolved by millennia of acid rain, leaving behind sediments that oxidize to a red color and create a soil called terra rossa. The sediments erode into the valleys as they form, creating secondary deposits that can be many meters deep. Small amounts of red wind-blown dust (called loess) blow north from the Sahara desert as well, adding a fine-grained additional component to the local sediments, particularly along the southern coast of the island. The Cretan terra rossa contains a substantial amount of kaolinite clay (between 30% and 59% according to Morris 2002, 56). Its other constituents include large percentages of quartz and other tiny grains that are not plastic, so by itself this red clay is only suitable for making items that do not require much manipulation by the potters, like bricks.

The second class of clay formed as marine deposits. The sediments were created in shallow water under the sea beginning during the Miocene period (Fassoulas 2001). These clays are very pale colored, and they include large amounts of calcium carbonate from the remains of marine shells as well as clay minerals. Except in rare instances (Blitzer 1984, 145–146), the traditional potters of Crete were unable to use any of these clays by themselves, because they were too sticky and too plastic.

An important lesson from the traditional pottery industry of Crete for our understanding of Early Minoan ceramics is that clays were routinely blended. The simple solution for the two raw materials—one too stiff and the other too plastic—was to mix them together. For the making of vessels, the traditional potters almost always used only blends of clays that combined the red terra rossa with the white marine clay. Different proportions were used depending on the character of the individual clay deposits that were available and the kind of vessel that was being made. Hand methods required more terra rossa to make the vase hold its shape better during drying, while work on the potter's wheel was facilitated by a more plastic blend. Larger shapes held their shape better if they were stiffer, and vases designed to withstand heat also needed more terra rossa to make them more porous and reduce the expansion during heating. Because the EM I potters had to use the same raw materials as more recent craftsmen, their solution to the same problem was also similar. The microscopic examination of Early Minoan pottery finds abundant evidence for the mixing of clays.

A second important conclusion from the traditional potters that bears on our understanding of EM I pottery has to do with the availability of suitable raw materials. The distribution patterns for regions in the world with so few clay sources that only a few workshops are possible are very different from regions where deposits of raw materials are plentiful. The ease of availability of good clays can have a positive effect on the existence of household productions and other small workshops with limited goals.

The documentation of over 130 temporary workshops set up by the potters from Thrapsano provides a partial picture of the distribution of modern clay sources in Crete (Psaropoulou 1996, 113–121). In spite of the need for two different types of clay deposits by the Thrapsaniote potters, they could set up their operations all over the island. Even after thousands of years of exploiting Crete's clays, good deposits are still abundant and widely distributed. The EM I potters will have had no difficulty in finding suitable materials for their nascent industry.

The same island-wide distribution of the Thrapsaniote workshops also gives some idea of the extensive need for clay vases in an agrarian society from the years before the use of plastics and other materials for waterproof and vermin-proof containers. In spite of the presence of metal and glass, clay vessels were still preferred for many uses. The large jars made by the traditional potters held many things in addition to foods, especially clothing, blankets, and other items made of cloth that could be damaged by insects. Large clay vessels were routinely used in many households (Christakis 2005, 64–69).

The EM I Fabrics

Fabrics provide an important tool for the modern researcher who wants to organize the ancient material by a characteristic based on the original place of manufacture or who wishes to assign vases to their places of origin. In a few cases, the inclusions are derived from a specific geological environment with limited distribution, and the origin can be documented. In other cases, even if the source cannot be known with certainty (the difficulty is compounded by the mixing of clays from more than one source), the use of a particular recipe for vases allows vessels with similar fabrics to be put in the same category, so that relationships can be established based on place of manufacture or geological region. The organization of classes based on fabrics provides a useful complement to the classifications based on other characteristics like methods of manufacture, shape, and style of decoration.

A few of the EM I fabrics are distinctive enough to be recognized even without petrographic analysis. In other cases, only examination under the microscope can reveal enough information for proper classification. Sometimes a group of fabrics can be recognized without magnification, but when the same large inclusions were added to different clay bases (whose character is too small to be seen with the unaided eye), the subvarieties cannot be distinguished without microscopic examination.

The following examples are particularly distinctive, and they are common in EM I. Several others exist as well.

CALCITE-TEMPERED FABRIC GROUP

Large fragments of bright white calcite or marble were used as temper in several different production centers. An example is shown in Figure 3.1. The white material is crystallized calcium carbonate ($CaCO_3$), which could have been collected in Crete either from the calcite veins in the dark gray limestone called Plattenkalk or from the phacoids of marble that occur at many locations. The mineral species in both of these rocks is calcite, even though the geology of the two sources is very different (the dark limestone is part of the African tectonic plate, while the phacoids, which are blocks of rock removed from their original places of formation, were pushed to Crete by the movement of the European tectonic plate). The term Calcite-Tempered Fabric Group is preferred here, because the temper was added to several different clay bases. In addition to its use in Crete, this recipe was popular for ceramic pastes in the Cyclades (Vaughan 1990) as well as on the Greek mainland (Vaughan, Myer, and Betancourt 1995, Crushed Calcite Group). It has been noted from several

Figure 3.1. Large white fragments of calcite are easily visible within the fabric of this conical pyxis with interior divisions from Hagia Photia Siteias, Tomb 27, HNM 3653 (photograph by Chronis Papanikolopoulos). Ht. 7.5 cm.

sites in Crete (Day 1991, 97; Vaughan 2002, 152; Day, Joyner, and Relaki 2003, 18–19).

Because this material was readily available, and the calcite was stable below ca. 650–850°C, it was popular in the low-fired ceramics of the Neolithic. It continued to be used in the EM I fabrics of the Coarse Dark Burnished Class, and it was also used for several other classes. The white carbonate was monocrystalline (Day, Joyner, and Relaki 2003, 18–19). It was usually angular from crushing by the potters. These inclusions cannot be used with high-fired ceramics. They are easily visible in the fired clay, especially if the fabric is dark. In most cases, these fabrics are low-fired, because if the kiln gets too hot, the calcite breaks down with released carbon dioxide that can force small chips to break off near the inclusions (called spalling) or even cause the vase to crack. The Calcite-Tempered Fabric Group is always coarse in texture, but the fired clay can vary greatly in color, from reddish yellow to red to brown to black, depending on the firing conditions.

ANGULAR RED INCLUSIONS FABRIC GROUP

A fabric with angular red inclusions is used for a substantial amount of EM I pottery, including pithoi (Fig. 3.2). The red material is not identified with

Figure 3.2. Angular red inclusions are visible on the surface of this sherd from Aphrodite's Kephali, AK 38. Size of field ca. 3 cm.

certainty. It is always angular from crushing, and it is different from the elongated and flattened fragments of red phyllite that are also used during this period. The red material is extremely fine grained, with both clay-sized and silt-sized grains. The reddish brown to red color is derived from hematite. Textures for the fabric as a whole vary from medium coarse to coarse, and colors vary from pale to red to dark, depending on the firing conditions.

MIRABELLO FABRIC

Mirabello Fabric is defined by the presence of an igneous suite of minerals derived from rocks in the diorite to granodiorite range. Descriptions of the fabric have been published many times (Myer in Betancourt et al. 1979, 4; Myer, McIntosh, and Betancourt 1995, 144–145; Day 1991, 92–94; 1997, 225; Whitelaw et al. 1997, 268; Vaughan 2002, 153–154; Barnard 2003, 7; Day, Joyner, and Relaki 2003, 17–18; Day et al. 2005, 183–187). In the system devised for Kavousi based on macroscopic examination, this fabric includes Types 2 and 3 (Haggis and Mook 1993; Haggis 2005, 169). Diorite is a granular igneous rock consisting principally of plagioclase feldspar, an amphibole mineral, and a dark mica, while granodiorite has a small percentage of K-feldspar as well as the plagioclase and more quartz than occurs in the diorite (Hurlbut and Klein 1977, 458, 460).

Both rocks have been identified in Minoan pottery. The dark mica was formerly called biotite (now no longer considered a distinct species; see Back and Mandarino 2008, 25). It occurs as tiny plates that can provide bronzy sparkles when a sherd is examined in sunlight. With macroscopic examination, the plagioclase is bright white, and the amphibole is usually black. The minerals can occur either as rock fragments with two or all three constituents present or as isolated individual fragments. Because diorite and granodiorite only occur in Crete along the northeast coast in the region of the Gulf of Mirabello (Dierckx and Tsikouras 2007), this fabric can be used to identify the regional source for the vases that use it.

SOUTH COAST FABRIC GROUP

A fabric group from the south coast of Central Crete used a series of rock and mineral inclusions that included sedimentary, igneous, and metamorphic constituents, all in sub-rounded to rounded shapes indicating they came from secondary depositions. The fabric group was common in the Mesara, and it has been defined from that region and from the Myrtos area as well as from small numbers of sherds found elsewhere. Generally similar deposits of these weathered rocks occur along a long stretch of the south coast of Crete. They are especially visible in the sands on beaches and in streams, which are probably the sources for at least some of the temper used for this fabric group. The constituents were first identified from the variety used at Kommos (Myer and Betancourt 1990, 9–10), and the fabric group has been described in print several times since then (Wilson and Day 1994; Whitelaw et al. 1997, 268; Day et al. 2005, 187–189; Day, Relaki, and Faber 2006, 39–46). Sedimentary inclusions consist of sandstone, limestone, chert, and siltstone (Day, Relaki, and Faber 2006, 41; note that sources containing limestone are avoided in later recipes because of the danger of breaking). Igneous grains include fragments of granitic rocks (containing quartz, plagioclase, amphibole, and other constituents), monocrystalline quartz, and fine-grained igneous rocks (perhaps basalt or diabase, sometimes with inclusions of elongated hollow crystals of plagioclase feldspar). Many of the minerals are highly altered. The suite of metamorphic constituents is substantial: phyllite, schist, polycrystalline quartz, epidote, chlorite, serpentine, pyroxene, amphibole, and altered micas. Occasional inclusions of shell fragments occur in some samples. All the constituents are not visible in every sherd, because some of them are uncommon or rare.

The coarseness ranges from very coarse (with inclusions over a centimeter in size) to medium coarse to fine. The color is extremely variable because different clays were mixed for the recipe, and the potters varied the amounts of all the ingredients. Pale colors are common for transport, storage, and serving shapes, but some of the firings resulted in brown or red products. Fabrics used for cooking vessels regularly used large amounts of terra rossa in the clay mixtures, which resulted in reddish-brown to brownish-red to red colors.

PHYLLITE-TEMPERED FABRIC GROUP

Phyllite, the fine-grained altered shale with grain sizes between that of slate (which is finer) and schist (which is coarser), occurs in many parts of Crete, and it was regularly used as a temper in fabrics. It has been studied in greatest detail from sites using the outcrops on the eastern side of the Gulf of Mirabello (Day 1991, 96, 100, 104–105; Betancourt and Myer 1995; Myer, McIntosh, and Betancourt 1995, 144; Vaughan 2002, 147–149; Day, Joyner, and Relaki 2003, 14–17). In the macroscopic identification of fabrics from the Kavousi survey, this category is Type 1 (Haggis and Mook 1993; Haggis 2005, 168–169). Occasionally, the grain size is large enough for the included material to be called schist, and sometimes slate occurs as well. The rock fragments are made of altered quartz, feldspars, micas, amphiboles, pyroxenes, and numerous less common minerals. All of these rocks are metamorphic, with a lamellar (layered) appearance. The fragments in the clay are often visible as flattened and elongated grains. Colors of the fired clays are highly variable.

4

The Pottery Shapes

One of the most important parts of the new ceramic development in EM I was the use of a large selection of shapes that were new to Crete. These shapes were derived from several sources including older forms inherited from the Neolithic, shapes borrowed from other ceramic traditions, copies of vases made of other materials, ideas that were inspired by shapes seen in nature, and newly created designs the potters invented themselves. The result was a very rich tradition.

Ceramic vases often serve more than one purpose. First, of course, most of them have to be useful containers. Their success in this regard depends on how successfully the shape accommodates the special character of whatever is inside, including facilitating the removal of the contents as needed while also offering protection from loss or spoilage. Because of this aspect of vessel design, specific details are often planned to suit particular purposes. In addition to their use as containers, however, ceramic vases can have one or more other functions that differ from vessel to vessel and from culture to culture. In some cases, the products are art objects intended to be displayed and admired for their aesthetic qualities. In this role, they can be beautiful or interesting, or they can evoke memories or abstract concepts. The vases can act as labels to their contents, so that users or potential customers who recognize a container can be aware of what it contains. Ceramics can also have symbolic meaning. By alluding to ideas or events the user of the vase already knows, a vessel can evoke ideas by extension. The thoughts inspired by the vase can be charged with religious meaning, or they can recall a personal memory or refer to many other intangible ideas. Such aspects are probably especially important in connection with vases buried with the dead. Because of these complicated characteristics, ceramic vases can serve multiple functions. They can be kept on display in a house or public building, used in storage, shipped away from their region of manufacture as a gift or for exchange, offered to deities, or buried with the dead.

The vases of EM I can be divided into several different classes on the basis of shape. In several cases, a single shape was decorated in more than one ornamental style, suggesting that both the potters and their customers could conceive of at least some of the vessel forms independently of any particular class of decoration. The shapes can be divided into the following groups:

1. Deep Open Shapes (chalices, cups, deep bowls, goblets, kernoi, tripod cooking pots)

2. Shallow Open Shapes (cooking dishes, frying pans, shallow bowls, stands)

3. Closed Shapes (amphoras, bottles, jars, jugs, pithoi, pyxides, specialty vases, tankards)

4. Other Shapes (jars with cut-outs, lids)

Deep Open Shapes

Deep vessels with open rims are well suited to holding liquids for drinking. In EM I this class includes both large vessels that would hold enough beverage for several persons and small containers that are more suitable for individuals.

CHALICES

A chalice was a deep conical bowl supported on a conical base (Fig. 4.1). EM I chalice shapes were large enough to suggest the vase could have been used as a communal drinking vessel, and the exterior was often decorated with grooves or burnishing. The chalice was common in northern and eastern Crete but less popular in western and southern Crete. Chalices were already widely distributed in the eastern Mediterranean during the Neolithic period, including in the Aegean islands (Evans and Renfrew 1968, figs. 1–3), but they were not used in Crete until EM I. Both Cycladic chalices and local versions were used in the island.

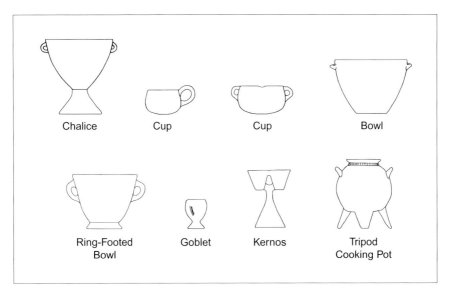

Figure 4.1. Deep open shapes. Not to scale.

CUPS

Relatively few simple cups with vertical handles were made in EM I (Fig 4.1), but the useful shape would become more common beginning in the next period. The bowl portion could be either rounded or conical. Some cups were given decorative horns on the rim, a detail inherited from the Neolithic. In addition to the one-handled shape, the cup was also made with two opposed handles.

DEEP BOWLS

Bowls were common in the Neolithic, and they continued to be made in EM I (Fig. 4.1). This was a utilitarian shape that was often undecorated. Profiles were usually rounded or straight rather than complex. Horizontal handles, flat tabs that rose above the vessel's rim, and simple lugs were all used for lifting. The Cycladic bowl shape with a tab handle was made in a continuous series from shallow to deep, so it was sometimes a good container for beverage, but shallow examples that would spill easily if used for liquids were made as well. A shape with a conical bowl on a low ring-base (the ring-footed bowl or chalice with low base) was an elegant drinking vessel made with thin walls and a carefully-made shape.

GOBLETS

The goblet with a small bowl supported on a stemmed base (Fig. 4.1) was an uncommon vessel in EM I. It would have been an individual drinking vessel, because EM I examples were small and would hold very little. The goblet was sometimes decorated with simple incised decoration.

KERNOI

A kernos is a multiple vessel (Fig. 4.1). EM I cups were sometimes joined together and given bases, forming kernoi. Such vases are awkward if used for drinking (if they are raised to the mouth and tilted, only one vessel touches the lips, and the others spill their contents) The kernoi are best suited to ceremonial purposes.

TRIPOD COOKING POTS

Because they were intended to be used over fires, cooking vessels supported on three legs were well-designed to allow the heating of their contents (Fig. 4.1). The shape was uncommon in EM I, and simple bowls and jars were also used for preparing food.

Shallow Open Shapes

Shallow vases with wide rims are most suitable for solid contents because liquids would spill easily from such vessels. The EM I shallow vases never have vertically placed loop handles, which are appendages that are well suited to lifting cups for drinking. The class includes both simple shapes and more complicated ones that may have served ceremonial functions.

COOKING DISHES

The cooking dish, also sometimes called a baking plate, was a shallow vessel with a rounded lower part (Fig. 4.2). Marks from burning are common on the shape, and it was surely used in preparing food. The walls were often extremely thin, suggesting that the dishes were probably kept in place in hearths and not moved very much. Foods that were cooked in such vessels probably included flat breads, because ovens were not present in Early Minoan Crete.

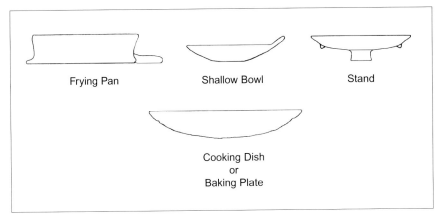

Figure 4.2. Shallow open shapes. Not to scale.

FRYING PANS

The Cycladic shape called the frying pan was a rare shape in Crete (Fig. 4.2). During EM I the shape was a shallow container with a flat base, low almost vertical sides, and a flat handle made as a horizontal tab that was an extension of the base. Most known Cretan examples were undecorated, but a few were given incised designs on the flat base. The EM I examples probably served as bowls (no examples are known with any signs of burning). They were too shallow for use with a beverage, because a liquid would spill easily.

SHALLOW BOWLS

Several types of bowls were made in EM I (Fig. 4.2). In many cases their exact purpose is unclear, and many of them could have had more than one function. Among the Cycladic designs that were used in Crete were bowls with tab handles. Like the frying pans that are closely related in style of decoration, the bowls with tab handles are somewhat enigmatic shapes whose use is not completely apparent from their form. They are often deep enough to have served as drinking vessels, but the open, shallow shape of some examples suggests they were at least sometimes used as containers for something that was not liquid.

STANDS

The Cretan stand (Fig. 4.2) consists of a shallow, flat-based dish supported on a centrally placed cylindrical base. The stand was first used in

EM I, and it continued to be used in EM IIA. The wide and shallow shape suggests it was designed to hold solid objects like food rather than liquids.

Closed Shapes

Deep shapes with lids or with constricted rims were suitable for shipping and storage. They were surely used for a wide variety of products, both liquid and solid. Many different types were used.

AMPHORAS

The amphora (Fig. 4.3) was a jar with opposed vertical handles. It usually had a somewhat constricted mouth to facilitate tight closure for shipping and storage. Amphoras were not common in EM I, and their role was often assumed by other types of shapes.

BOTTLES

The bottle (Fig. 4.3) circulated mostly in northern Crete. Its small mouth would have made it suitable only for liquids, and the narrow neck would have facilitated shipping because of the ease in closure. Both Cycladic bottles with incised decoration and Cretan examples with plain or burnished surfaces were used in EM I.

JARS

Jars are deep vessels with cylindrical or rounded bodies, handles for lifting, and an open or partially constricted mouth (Fig. 4.3). EM I jars were of many different types. If the vase has a cylindrical upper part that rises above the shoulder and functions as both neck and rim, the shape is called a collared jar (Fig. 4.3, upper right). The jar was a standard multipurpose container during the Neolithic, and the form continued into the Bronze Age. It was extremely common.

JUGS

A jug is a pouring vessel with one vertical handle opposite a spout (Fig. 4.3). Most EM I jugs were designed for both transport and serving. Their cylindrical necks could have been closed with stoppers carved from tree limbs, and their elevated spouts facilitated pouring. The spout was not used in Crete before EM I. The earliest spouted jugs in the island had rounded

Amphora Bottle Collared Jar

Jug Tankard Jar with Cut-Outs

Conical Pyxis Spherical Pyxis Biconical Pyxis Specialty Vase

Figure 4.3. Closed shapes. Not to scale.

bases and vertical or almost vertical spouts, which are features that suggest they were copied from vessels made from gourds (Hood 1971, 30). The Cretan gourd has a rounded part away from the stem and a more cylindrical part near the stem, so that it could be easily cut to make a jug with a rounded form and a vertical spout (Betancourt 1985, 23 and pl. 2a). The gourd-vases would not have been stable enough to rest on a flat surface, and if they were suspended by strings or nets, their Hagios Onouphrios Style decoration was perhaps also derived from the appearance of the hanging containers. Jugs with vertical spouts that resemble gourds occur in Anatolia as well as in Crete (Betancourt 1985, 26, fig. 15), and the shape need not have originated in the Aegean.

PITHOI

The EM I pithoi were the largest ceramic objects made at the beginning of the Cretan Bronze Age (Frontispiece). They had a rounded body and a cylindrical upper part that functioned as collar and rim. At least in some cases, the bases were rounded to facilitate tipping. The volume, ca. 165 kilograms in the largest known example, permitted bulk storage of either liquid or solid commodities.

PYXIDES

The pyxis, a small box with a lid, was an important EM I shape that was made in many varieties (Fig. 4.3). Rounded versions may have imitated the sea urchins that are so common in the Aegean (Doumas 1977, 16). Cylindrical and conical pyxides could reflect boxes carved from tree limbs. Rounded pyxides with central raised necks could have been based on small gourds. All of these boxes seem to have had lids, suggesting that if they were used for consumables the products were something that needed a wide mouth to remove the contents and a tight-fitting lid to keep the product safe (possibilities among food products could include runny cheese, butter, honey, and many other commodities, but perfumed unguents and ointments are also suitable for such vases). In many cases the lids and rims had matching holes so the pyxis could be hung up with cords, and the lid could slide up the strings to remove some of the contents and then slide back into place easily. A few examples exist that were manufactured as several pyxides joined together to make kernoi.

SPECIALTY VASES

Specialty vases (Fig. 4.3) are unusually shaped vessels whose form is either freshly created by the potters or adapted from something not usually regarded as a container. Some of the specialty vases are shaped like birds, animals, or other natural forms. Many of them are either unique or extremely rare. The vases are usually rather small, and most of them are known only from tombs. Many of the examples may have been created as special ceremonial pieces for use in funerary ceremonies.

TANKARDS

The tankard (Fig. 4.3) had a rounded or piriform shape, a mouth that was open enough from which to drink, and two opposed vertical handles. Like the EM I jug, its earliest examples have rounded bases, and the flat-based variety only developed later in the period. The shape was probably derived from gourds whose tops had been cut off to make drinking vessels (Betancourt 1985, pl. 2b). The elegant decoration and opposed handles, which were constant features, suggest that tankards may have played a role in drinking ceremonies in which the vessel was passed from one person to another.

Other Shapes

JARS WITH CUT-OUTS

The vessel with one handle and cut-outs (Fig. 4.3) is an Aegean shape, not a local Cretan one. Examples are known only from Minoan sites with close Cycladic connections. The shape consists of a closed vessel with a wide collar/rim pierced with triangular openings. It is assumed that a lamp or candle would have been placed inside to make the vase into a lantern or an incense burner. With this purpose, the solid lower part of the form would have protected the flame from the wind, and the cut-outs would have permitted the light to be seen or allowed the aroma to escape.

LIDS

The pyxides and a few other shapes had lids or covers (Fig. 4.3). They were often made with their vessels as a set to insure that the two pieces fitted together properly.

5

EM I Surface Treatments and Decoration and their Relation to Fabrics, Shapes, and Methods of Manufacture

Pottery was made in several ways during Early Minoan I. The diversity in final products suggests that this period was a time of experimentation when potters tried various approaches for the manufacture of ceramics. Vases could be fired either to make them dark or to achieve bright, pale colors. Sometimes the decoration modified the clay itself, while other systems applied painted designs in a different material on the surface. Although some of these ideas would be quickly abandoned, others would form the roots of the later Minoan development.

Only part of the EM I pottery can be easily distinguished from earlier and later chronological phases. The new phase following Final Neolithic is defined by the deposits at Knossos (Wilson 2007, 50) as well as by its style. It includes a specific set of pottery classes and fabrics, some of which are continuations or developments from the preceding period and others that are completely new. Among the new classes are the Hagios Onouphrios Style and the Lebena Style, neither of which is known from before the EM I period. Other typical classes include the Fine Dark Gray Burnished Class (with its pattern-burnished subvariety called the Pyrgos Style), the Scored Style, and a whole series of other, somewhat less distinctive groups of vases. New shapes appear in Crete at this time, with spouted jugs, several types of pyxides, and pithoi being especially important. The end of the phase is also recognizable, although the changes are more gradual. Among the new developments in EM IIA are the decline of the large chalice in preference for smaller goblets, a use of dark linear decoration that replaces the earlier red painting, and an increase of tighter, more controlled compositions. The Pyrgos Style continues for a while (Wilson 1985, 294), but it declines in popularity. New classes that begin before the end of EM I but become more common in EM IIA include the Fine Gray Style (also called Fine Gray Ware; for discussion, see Betancourt 1985, 40) and the Koumasa Style (for discussions, see Zois 1968 and Betancourt 1985, 40–43).

Within EM I, phasing is more difficult. Knossos does not have any published stratigraphic sequence of deposits from this period (for a possible unpublished instance, see Hood 2006, 12), and a well from this site seems to have distinct pottery because of its social use rather than because of a difference in time (Wilson and Day 2000, 51–53). An early and a later phase of EM I have also been recognized in south-central Crete (Warren 2004, 117–118, 194). General chronological indications show that the large assemblage from Hagia Photia is late within the period, because Fine Gray pottery has already appeared alongside the EM I vases (Davaras and Betancourt 2004, 57, 155, 190). Kephala Petras has two EM I phases, an earlier one without the Cycladic style vases and a later phase with them, which can divide the period for that site and for others that seem comparable. A precise division between EM IA and EM IB that will work for all of Crete, however, has not yet been defined.

Surface Treatments and Decorations

The character of EM I pottery was based on the materials that were chosen, the methods of manufacture, the shapes, the different surface treatments, and the firing technology. Potters made various decisions about which clay recipes to adopt, how to make and decorate the resulting vases, and what firing technology to use. The complex relationships between these independent variables resulted in a great diversity in the finished products.

The most distinctive classes of decoration during EM I include the following groups and styles.

COARSE DARK BURNISHED CLASS

The coarse-textured, dark burnished pottery of EM I was a direct continuation of the technology of the Final Neolithic, with the addition of some new shapes alongside the standard cups, bowls, and jars that continued to be popular. One of the advantages of the techniques used for the Neolithic pottery of Crete was that the simple steps in manufacture encouraged many different types of production centers, including some informal ones that probably made just a handful of vases for a small group of people in a family or small settlement. For the simplest vases, clays were dug from nearby clay pits or outcrops and combined with locally available stones and organic matter to make a porous, coarse clay mixture. Vessels were modeled by hand from slabs or pieces of clay into simple bowls and rounded jars and then rubbed hard while they were still moist to compress the surface (burnishing). After they dried thoroughly, the vases could be made permanently hard by heating them for many hours in any enclosed space that would hold the heat, like a pit, a hearth, or even an open fire where the vases were stacked on the ground and surrounded by fuel that was set on fire and allowed to burn with much addition of fuel over the course of many hours. Covering the fire (as in charcoal making) was also possible.

Shapes like those in Figure 5.1 used the Final Neolithic ceramic practices. They could have been made in a household setting that worked at pottery making only intermittently in order to supply local needs or in a more formal and professional workshop staffed by full-time potters. With a range of different types of FN productions, it is not surprising that some of the workshops would survive well into EM I and continue to make conservative products. The vases in Figure 5.1 have dark colors throughout their fabrics as well as black and burnished exterior surfaces, showing that they were fired in an enclosed space that did not allow any air to enter. Their shapes are fairly simple.

The bowl with an inward-leaning rim that creates a constricted mouth (Fig. 5.1B) has parallels from the northeast Aegean. Examples come from Kum Tepe IB (Sperling 1976, figs. 13–15), Emporio VIII–X (Hood 1981–1982, I, fig. 143, no. 468, and fig. 144, nos. 504, 509, and 520), Poliochni Black phase (Bernabò-Brea 1964–1976, I, pl. 5b, c) and Poliochni Blue phase (Bernabò-Brea 1964–1976, I, pl. 9e–h). The parallels have a similar black-burnished appearance and a similar form, but whether the resemblance is accidental or not is uncertain because the shape is simple, and the black-burnished technology is widely distributed.

The Coarse Dark Burnished Class was especially popular in northeast Crete. At some sites in that region like Mochlos, it was almost the exclusive pottery that was used (Seager 1912, 92–97). The vases must have been made at several different locations, because they come in many fabrics, though the use of the Calcite-Tempered Fabric Group and the Phyllite-Tempered Fabric Group seem to have been especially popular.

By the end of the period, some of the workshops making this class had learned to fire their burnished vessels in a kiln, producing a much better

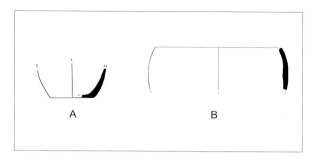

Figure 5.1. Simple bowls and jars, Coarse Dark Burnished Class, FN–EM I. A. Pacheia Ammos Rock Shelter, PAR 46 (courtesy of Stavroula Apostolakou and Thomas Brogan). B. Pseira, Tomb 7, INSTAP-SCEC, PS 2343. Scale 1:6.

product than could be made in a simple pit or covered fire. These vases are recognizable by their red or reddish-yellow fabrics, which contrast with the more conservative surfaces that are sometimes still black and heavily burnished. The fabric color shows that the vases were fired in a kiln with abundant oxygen. The surface would still become black if the potters closed their kiln at the end of the firing cycle, briefly creating the reducing atmosphere that made the surface black and (if the temperature reached the sintering point) trapping the black color below the sintered slip, even when the kiln was opened again to cool it off.

Shapes that are more complex than simple rounded bowls and jars, with specialized and carefully made details, were occasionally produced in the Coarse Dark Burnished Class, suggesting that some formal workshops made this pottery. Several types of goblet are among the shapes that were developed in EM I (Fig. 5.2). They consist of a cup supported on a stem or low base, with individual details for the shape of the bowl, the type of foot below the stem, and the exact shape of the stem itself. Occasionally, these vases are decorated with incised lines (Fig. 5.2B). The vases in Figure 5.2 all come from East Crete, but the goblet also occurs at Debla in West Crete (Warren and Tzedhakis 1974, 323), demonstrating that the distribution extended throughout the island.

An early version of a stand from Knossos is also made in this class of pottery (Fig. 5.3). It is an early, shallow version of a shape that would become more popular in EM IIA. A cylindrical stand was used to support a shallow bowl with a flat base and low sides. The stand's surface was black and glossy from hard burnishing, while the core was a dark red. The EM IIA stands of this type continued this tradition into the next period. They were made in one or more workshops in the Pediada or Lasithi, and they were traded to many sites in central and eastern Crete. In EM IIA, the shape was used especially for offerings in tombs.

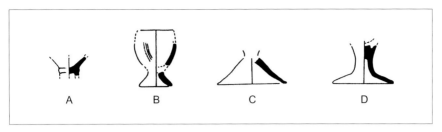

Figure 5.2. Specialized goblet shapes, Coarse Dark Burnished Class, EM I. A. Hagios Charalambos Cave, INSTAP-SCEC, HCH 149. B. Hagia Photia Siteias, Tomb 28, HNM unnumbered. C. Kalo Chorio (after Haggis 1996, 665, fig. 23, no. KT 24). D. Pseira, Tomb 1, INSTAP-SCEC, PS 1307 (after Betancourt and Davaras, eds., 2003, fig. 22, no. 1.37). Scale 1:6.

Figure 5.3. A. EM I stand from Knossos (after Hood 1990a, fig. 2, no. 18). B. EM I–IIA stand from Hagios Charalambos, HNM 12,580 (drawing courtesy of Louise Langford-Verstegen). Scale 1:6.

HAGIOS ONOUPHRIOS STYLE

In contrast with the Coarse Dark Burnished Class, which can be regarded as a continuation of Final Neolithic ways of making ceramics, the Hagios Onouphrios Style, also called Hagios Onouphrios Ware (Davaras 1976, 135–136), represents an adoption of the entire new technology of EM I. The style uses red linear decoration on a pale background to decorate a specific group of shapes (Figs. 2.2, 5.4). It has sometimes been called Dark-on-Light Painted Ware (Wilson and Day 2000, 33), but this is a misnomer because the term Hagios Onouphrios has been in the literature longer (Branigan 1970a, 126), and the proposed new name does not distinguish between vases with red or with brown to black ornament. The decoration of the Hagios Onouphrios Style is always red. This distinction between the colors is a crucial characteristic because the difference is caused by a specific change in technology. For the red color, the kiln is kept open, creating ferric oxide in the slip. To create the dark color of the ornament in contrast with a pale background, the potters had to adopt a complex three-stage firing system. The kiln was first kept open to admit oxygen while the vase was fired to a temperature just below the sintering point. The potters would then close the doors of the kiln just before the temperature reached this stage, creating a reducing atmosphere that changed the red ferric oxide to black ferrous oxide. The iron oxide changed chemically and turned dark in the presence of carbon monoxide, and with sintering enhanced by the fluxing action of the reducing atmosphere, the dark colors were trapped below the vitrified surface of the slip before the potters again opened the door of the kiln to re-admit oxygen and re-oxidize the vases to restore the pale colored surfaces of the body (but not the vitrified slip). The new technique, with a long later history into the Classical Greek period and beyond it (Noble 1988, 80), began to be used in Crete during EM I, but it was not practiced in all workshops. Using it was a deliberate decision. Vases with dark linear ornament are better called the Koumasa Style, reserving the term Hagios

Figure 5.4. Hagios Onouphrios Style jug from Hagia Photia Siteias, Tomb 195, HNM 4197 (photograph by Chronis Papanikolopoulos). Ht. 23.5 cm.

Onouphrios Style for the vases with red linear designs on a pale background.

The style uses a large percentage of calcareous Neogene clays (early to middle Miocene in date), producing a pale fabric. The vessels are fired to a higher temperature (ca. 850–1050°C) than the Coarse Dark Burnished Class as established by SEM analysis (Kilikoglou in Wilson and Day 1994), which is the stable range caused by the high calcareous content (Maniatis and Tite 1981). This pale color contrasts nicely with the dark red paint used for decoration. If a ware is defined as a specific style used with a particular fabric or fabric group, two specific wares have been defined:

1. South Coast Hagios Onouphrios Ware, using the style with pottery made in the South Coast Fabric Group, a fabric from South Crete that was also imported into Knossos (Wilson and Day 1994, 69)

2. Angular Red Inclusions Hagios Onouphrios Ware, made in the Fabric with Angular Red Inclusions (discussed below)

The fine quality of this class of pottery can be seen in the first complete example to be discovered in modern times, the jug from Hagios Onouphrios shown in Figure 2.2 that gives its name to the style. The vase has a rounded base, a globular body, and an elevated spout. Like many of the best examples of this ware, the surface was covered with a white slip before the decoration was applied. Carefully painted red lines sweep around the vase, emphasizing its volume. The design is conceived as a three dimensional composition. Spout and handle divide the vase into two halves, and similar decoration is placed on each side. This design concept, already established here in EM I, would be used throughout the Minoan period. The choice of specific materials and the use of sophisticated firing technology have been used to suggest that the pottery was made by specialized potters (Day, Wilson, and Kiriatzi 1997, 281).

A selection of other Hagios Onouphrios Style vases can be seen in Figures 5.5 to 5.8. The examples in Figure 5.5 illustrate some of the changes that occurred in the style during the long EM I period. Although a precise division between the phases cannot be pinpointed for every type of vase, some changes did occur. The early EM I vessels have rounded profiles and rounded bases; the later vases have more piriform (pear-shaped) shapes and flat bases. At the beginning of EM I, many vases were designed to be hung from a high peg or beam to keep mice and other rodents away from them. This aspect of the design of the early tankards and jugs may also reflect the forms' antecedents (Hood 1990a, 370). A rounded gourd with a long neck could have been easily cut to make a round-bottomed

Figure 5.5. Hagios Onouphrios Style vases illustrating the stylistic changes during EM I from vases with globular bodies and rounded bottoms from early in the period (A and C) to taller forms with piriform bodies and flat bases late in the period (B and D). A. Jug from Lebena, Tomb II, HM 15,384 (drawing by Elizabeth Warren, inked by Susan Grice, after Warren 2004, fig. 21, no. 96). B. Jug from Hagia Photia Siteias, Tomb 202, HNM 4335, courtesy of the Hagia Photia project, Temple University. C. Tankard from Lebena, Tomb II, HM 15,322 (drawing by Elizabeth Warren, inked by Susan Grice, after Warren 2004, fig. 30, no. 437. D. Tankard from Hagia Photia Siteias, Tomb 96, HNM 3617, courtesy of the Hagia Photia project, Temple University. Scale 1:6.

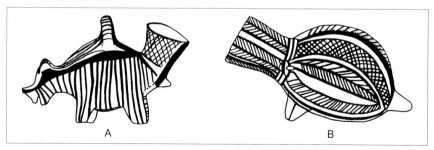

Figure 5.6. Specialty vases made in the Hagios Onouphrios Style, from Lebena, Tomb II. A. Small quadruped, HM 15,368. B. Animal with legs and a tail and a raised bar along the back (wild boar?), HM 15,399 (drawings by Elizabeth Warren, inked by Susan Grice, after Warren 2004, fig. 31, nos. 507 [a] and 508 [b]). Scale 1:3.

container with a vertical spout—only a handle would need to be added after trimming off the neck to complete a high-spouted jug. The vessels fashioned from gourds, like the clay vases copied from them, would have rounded bases, so they could not rest on a flat surface. If they were used as storage vessels, they could be firmly closed by inserting wooden plugs into the cylindrical necks.

The distribution of the Hagios Onouphrios Style covers all of Crete (see p. 52). More than one production center manufactured these vases. Examples made with the fabric containing angular red inclusions, almost certainly made somewhere in eastern Crete, are known both from Kephala Petras (Y. Papadatos, pers. comm.) and from Aphrodite's Kephali, and vases made in different fabrics are known from the Mesara and elsewhere. This evidence indicates that both vases and the ideas about how to make and decorate them traveled between the various production centers in Crete. The other vases include some cleverly molded small animals (Fig. 5.6), collared jars with knobs on the shoulders (Fig. 5.7), and a small vase shaped like a barrel (Fig. 5.8).

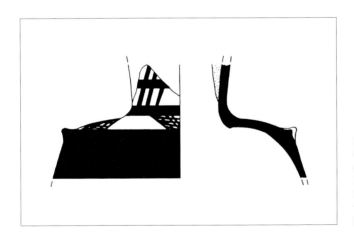

Figure 5.7. Hagios Onouphrios Style collared jar from Kalo Chorio (after Haggis 1996, 664, fig. 20, no. KT 1). Scale 1:3.

Figure 5.8. Hagios Onouphrios Style barrel vase (HM 4162) from Koumasa (after Zois 1968, pl. 22).

Sites with the Hagios Onouphrios Style

Alykomouri (Haggis 2005, 49); *Amnissos Cave* ("Eileithyia Cave") (Marinatos 1929a, fig. 1, lower row, nos. 1, 2); *Archanes* (Papadatos 2005, 14); *Chomatas*, near Kavousi (Day et al. 2005, 195); *Gournia* (Hawes et al. 1908, color pl. A, no. 3); *Hagia Kyriaki* (Blackman and Branigan 1982, 29–32; Vasilakis 1989–1990, pl. 6c); *Hagia Photia Siteias* (Davaras and Betancourt 2004, passim); *Hagia Triada* (La Rosa 1988, pl. 13c; Laviosa 1972–1973); *Hagia Triada Site B22* (Watrous and Hadzi-Vallianou 2004, 536); *Hagios Antonios* (Haggis 2005, 49); *Hagios Ioannis Site A72* (Watrous and Hadzi-Vallianou 2004, 533); *Hagios Ioannis Site B43* (Watrous and Hadzi-Vallianou 2004, 538); *Hagios Vasileos* near Petrokephali (Watrous and Hadzi-Vallianou 2004, 532); *Hagios Onouphrios* (Evans 1895; Watrous and Hadzi-Vallianou 2004, 532); *Kalamaki* (Hope Simpson 1995, 369); *Kalivia* (Watrous and Hadzi-Vallianou 2004, 537); *Kalo Chorio* (Haggis 1996, passim); *Knossos* (Hood 1966; Wilson and Day 2000, 33–39); *Koryphes* (Hope Simpson 1995, 376); *Koumasa* (Xanthoudides 1924, pl. 27, no. 4148); *Koutsokeras* (Xanthoudides 1924, 75); *Krasi* (Marinatos 1929b, figs. 9, no. 9, and 10, no. 2); *Kyparissi Cave*, at Kanli Kastelli (Alexiou 1951, pls. 13, 14); *Langos* (Hope Simpson 1995, 375); *Lebena* (Alexiou and Warren 2004, passim); *Loures*, near Hagios Ioannis (Watrous and Hadzi-Vallianou 2004, 533); *Malia* (van Effenterre and van Effenterre 1969, pl. 2); *Megaloi Skinoi*, near Hagia Kyriaki (Alexiou 1967, 482); *Patrikies* (Watrous and Hadzi-Vallianou 2004, 536); *Phaistos* (Pernier 1935, 130; Levi 1976, pls. 12, 13a–c, color pl. 4p, q); *Phaistos Site B27* (Watrous and Hadzi-Vallianou 2004, 537); *Phaistos Site B44* (Watrous and Hadzi-Vallianou 2004, 539); *Platyvola Cave* (Tzedakis 1966, pl. 466, no. 3); *Poros-Katsambas* (Wilson and Day 2000, 53; Wilson, Day, and Dimopoulou-Rethemiotaki 2004, 69); *Pseira* (Betancourt, Dierckx, and Reese 2003, 12, nos. 1.57, 1.58, and 37, nos. 3.9, 3.10); *Pyrgos Cave* (Xanthoudides 1918a, 144, fig. 5, nos. 5, 6, and pl. 1, upper left); *Selli* (Hope Simpson 1995, 378); *Sendones* (Hope Simpson 1995, 373; Betancourt 1995, 381); *Sivas* (Watrous and Hadzi-Vallianou 2004, 540); *Stravomytis Cave*, near Archanes (Sakellarakis and Sapouna-Sakellaraki 1997, 377, fig. 330); *Vigles* (Hope Simpson 1995, 360).

The barrel vase consists of a horizontal cylinder with a small neck at the top and its ends closed, with the vase supported on three tiny feet. It comes from Koumasa. The piece was once regarded as Middle Minoan I (Zervos 1956, 215, fig. 267), but the discovery of two examples in Tomb II at Lebena, one made in the Hagios Onouphrios Style and the other in the Lebena Style (Warren 2004, 62–63), show that this shape circulated in EM I. The shape is one of the forms with parallels from the northeast Aegean. Examples of barrel vases are known from Troy (Blegen et al. 1950, pl. 231a–b), Thermi (Lamb 1936, fig. 37, no. 367), and Poliochni on Lesbos (Bernabò-Brea 1964–1976, I, pl. 148a–b). Although the shape may originally be foreign, the painted ornament is purely Cretan. As in most cases, the Minoan potters transformed what they received from abroad to give it a new appearance.

The painted style is completely new in Crete. Its origins are uncertain, but both Egypt and Palestine have been proposed, because red-painted designs are known from there (Weinberg 1965, 307). Most of the other aspects of ceramic production in these regions, however, are not similar to Cretan practices.

Details on the finished products reveal that these vases were made using all the new EM I technology: a pale fabric from the choice of marl clays for the main part of the fabric recipe, new shapes including the use of tall spouts, a thin, hard wall from the high temperature made possible by the kiln, and carefully applied ornament in dark red slip reflecting the oxidizing atmosphere while the vases were being fired.

LEBENA STYLE

The same materials used for the Hagios Onouphrios Style were used for the Lebena Style (see p. 55 for sites), but the colors of the ornament were reversed (Fig. 5.9). The iron-rich red slip was used to cover the exterior surface, and the white slip that acted as a background on many Hagios Onouphrios Style vessels was used for the ornament. The resulting decoration had white designs on a red background.

The date for the style is established by several sites. At Hagia Photia, it occurs in the same tombs with the other EM I vessels (Davaras and Betancourt 2004). It was stratified below a level from EM IIA in Tomb II at Lebena (Alexiou and Warren 2004). A find at Marathokephalo along with EM IIA pottery suggests the possibility that it survives into the next period (discussion by Branigan 1970a, 28).

Figure 5.9. Tankard from Lebena, made in the Lebena Style, Tomb II, HM 15,373 (drawing by Elizabeth Warren, inked by Susan Grice, after Warren 2004, fig. 30, no. 454). Scale 1:3.

Figure 5.10. Lebena Style pyxis with an elliptical shape from Hagios Onouphrios, HM 7 (photograph by Chip Vincent). Length 15 cm.

A

B

Figure 5.11. Specialty vases made in the Lebena Style. A. Oval-shaped vase in the form of a gourd, from Lebena, Tomb II, HM 15,391. B. Small bottle from Lebena, Tomb II, HM 15,372 (drawings by Elizabeth Warren, inked by Susan Grice, after Warren 2004, fig. 32, no. 511 [a], and fig. 22, no. 145 [b]). Scale 1:3.

The Hagios Onouphrios Style and the Lebena Style were decorated using the same two materials, but some different preferences for shapes exist between the two classes. Hagios Onouphrios Style ornament was especially popular for jugs and tankards, and it was occasionally used for a wide variety of other forms. The Lebena Style was used for a wide variety of vases including a few tankards (Fig. 5.9) and some specialty shapes (Figs. 5.10, 5.11), but jugs were not usually decorated in this way. The obviously deliberately planned distinction tells us a great amount about the way that these early wares were intended to be understood. The decoration must have been a guide to the contents, acting as a label for whatever was inside the vases, and Lebena Style vessels did not contain what was shipped in the Hagios Onouphrios Style jugs.

The Lebena Style shapes are creative and extremely varied, with many unique pieces. A small pyxis that once had a lid comes from Hagios Onouphrios (Fig. 5.10). It has an elliptical shape and a pronounced shoulder with a raised neck where its lid would be fitted. Doubly-pierced lugs finish the design. The decoration is in the rectilinear system that is especially popular during this period, with bands and a zigzag motif. A small container in the shape of a gourd (Fig. 5.11A) has a handle at one end. Simple white bands are the only ornament. Vertical stripes enhance a small bottle (Fig. 5.11B). All of these vases are miniature containers with small necks designed for small amounts of some commodity that needed to be poured out only a little at a time. It is possible that they held perfumed oil or some other precious liquid.

Sites with the Lebena Style

Hagia Kyriaki (Blackman and Branigan 1982, 29); *Hagia Photia Siteias* (Davaras and Betancourt 2004, passim); *Hagios Onouphrios* (Evans 1895, 115; Betancourt 1985, pl. 2g; Watrous and Hadzi-Vallianou 2004, 530); *Knossos* (Evans 1903–1904, 22); *Koumasa* (Xanthoudides 1924, pl. 28, no. 4295); *Lebena* (Alexiou and Warren 2004, passim); *Marathokephalo* (Xanthoudides 1918b, 18); *Phaistos* (Pernier 1935, 130; Levi 1976, pl. 12k); *Sivas* (Paribeni 1913, 22, no. 35); *Stravomytis Cave*, near Archanes (Sakellarakis and Sapouna-Sakellaraki 1997, 378).

FINE DARK GRAY BURNISHED CLASS, INCLUDING THE PYRGOS STYLE

The Fine Dark Gray Burnished Class uses only some of the new ideas in pottery making that were becoming current in EM I. The potters who made these ceramic products used clay recipes with a large percentage of non-calcareous clays, but they made fine-grained and thin vases that were finished with great care. The vases must come from more than one workshop, because some of them are fired only to low temperatures, while others are harder and more durable (see list of sites, p. 59). The pieces found at Knossos were fired in kilns that were closed at the end of the firing to create the dark gray surfaces (Wilson and Day 1994, 71–72). Perhaps because the vases were uniformly dark, and painted lines would not show up well, this class was either left undecorated, or it received only grooves or other modifications to the surface, including designs made with the burnishing tool.

When the vases have burnished designs, they are called the Pyrgos Style (also called Pyrgos Ware). A fragment from Knossos (Fig. 5.12) illustrates how the lines of compressed surface show up in contrast with the unburnished parts of the vase. This vase is a chalice, a large drinking vessel that would hold enough beverage for several people.

The inventory of shapes is very different from the one used by the potters who made the Hagios Onouphrios Style. The chalice is certainly the most dramatic shape (Fig. 5.13). It consists of a conical open vessel of substantial size supported on a tall conical base. Some of the vases are over 20 cm high and fired hard. Many of them are decorated with burnished patterns made by rubbing to make individual lines instead of covering the entire vase with an even coating. The choice of a decorative system is interesting, in that it involves taking an aspect of the manufacturing process that had once been necessary to make the vase serviceable (but was now no longer needed because the vases were fired to higher temperatures) and using it for ornament.

Figure 5.12. Fragment of a chalice from Knossos (after Betancourt 1985, pl. 2H). Ht. 10 cm.

Chalices come in a wide range of shapes and sizes (Fig. 5.14). A selection of rims from Kalo Chorio (Fig. 5.15) illustrates the range from a single site. The vase was very popular, and it was used in many parts of Crete (it is rare or missing from many sites in the Mesara). A function as a communal drinking vessel has been proposed (Wilson and Day 2000), and this purpose seems correct both because of the large size of the drinking bowl and because of the archaeological contexts. The chalice is especially found in contexts suggesting drinking ceremonies, including those that accompanied funerals. At the Hagia Photia cemetery, chalices were found smashed on top of several of the graves, as if a final toast to the deceased was followed by breaking the vessel over the tomb (Davaras and Betancourt 2004, passim). Probably the attractive large vases were displayed during the burial ceremony and then used for the mourners from which to drink as a commemoration of the deceased.

The large drinking vessel on an elevated base was not invented in Crete. Many examples come from the northeast Aegean, and they are often dark and burnished like those from Crete (see the list of sites with the shape published by Mellaart 1966, 114). Especially good comparisons for the Cretan examples come from Beşik Tepe and Samos (Lamb 1932, 124–129, fig. 13), from Poliochni on Lemnos (Bernabò-Brea 1964–1976, I, pls. 9–22, 106–113), and from Kum Tepe IA and IB (Sperling 1976, with a list of other sites given on 316, n. 7). The finds from northwestern Anatolia and

Figure 5.13. Chalices made in the Fine Dark Gray Burnished Class, from Hagia Photia Siteias (photographs by Chronis Papanikolopoulos). Left: Tomb 226, HNM 2885, ht. 24.2 cm. Right: Tomb 134, HNM 4157, ht. 23.6 cm.

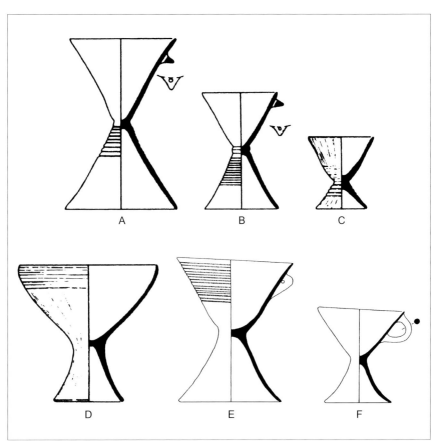

Figure 5.14. Chalices of several sizes. A–C. From the Pyrgos Cave (after Hood 1971, fig. 14, nos. 2, 3, 4). D. From Knossos (after Hood 1971, fig. 14, no. 1). E–F. From Hagia Photia Siteias. Scale 1:6.

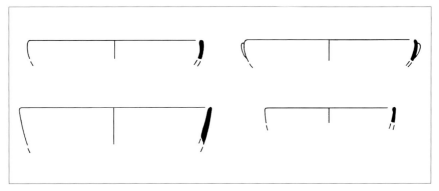

Figure 5.15. Variations in chalice rims from Kalo Chorio (after Haggis 1996, 665, fig. 22, nos. KT 13–KT 16). Scale 1:6.

Sites with the Pyrgos Style

Alykomouri (Haggis 2005, 49); *Amnissos Cave* ("Eileithyia Cave") (Marinatos 1929a, 96, fig. 1, center row, no. 2; 1930, 95, fig. 6); *Archanes* (Papadatos 2005, 13); *Arkalochori* (Hazzidakis 1912–1913, fig. 3); *Chrysokamino Cave*, also called *Theriospelio Cave* (Betancourt 1983, nos. 13–14; Haggis 2005, 49); *Chomatas*, near Kavousi (Day et al. 2005, 195); *Gortyn* (Levi 1965, 226); *Grimani Cave*, near Trapeza (Pendlebury, Pendlebury, and Money-Coutts 1937–1938a, 18, fig. 7, no. N21, and pl. 5.1, no. 21); *Hagia Kyriaki* (Blackman and Branigan 1978, 631; 1982, 27–29), *Hagia Photia Siteias* (Davaras and Betancourt 2004, passim); *Hagia Triada* (La Rosa 1988, pl. 13b; Todaro 2001, 17, fig. 7); *Hagios Onouphrios* (Watrous and Hadzi-Vallianou 2004, 530); *Kalo Chorio* (Haggis 1996, 664–666); *Kavousi village* (Haggis 2005, 49); *Knossos* (Evans 1921–1935, II, figs. 3m, 4; J.D. Evans 1964, 194; Hood 1961–1962, 93; 1966, 110; 1971, 38, fig. 14; 1990a, 369, fig. 1, nos. 1, 2; Wilson 1985, 297–299; Wilson and Day 2000, 27–33), *Kommos* (Betancourt 1990, nos. 1902–1906); *Korphi tou Koukkogianne*, at Ellenes (Marinatos 1932, col. 177); *Koutsokeras* (Xanthoudides 1924, 75); *Krasi* (Marinatos 1929b, fig. 17, upper row, no. 2); *Kyparissi Cave*, *Kanli Kastelli* (Alexiou 1951, pl. 14, fig. 1, nos. 2, 4, 5, and fig. 2, no. 7); *Lebena* (Alexiou and Warren 2004, passim); *Lera Cave* (Karantzali 1996, 86); *Mariyalles Cave*, near Ellenes (Marinatos 1933, col. 296); *Megaloi Skinoi*, near Hagia Kyriaki (Alexiou 1967, 482); *Partira* (Zervos 1956, fig. 119; Mortzos 1972); *Patrikies* (Bonacasa 1967–1968, 47); *Phaistos* (Pernier 1935, pl. 12, nos. 1, 6; Levi 1961–1962, figs. 132–133; 1964, 4–5; 1965; 1976, 281, 536, pl. 14; Vagnetti 1972–1973, type G); *Platyvola Cave* (Tzedakis 1967, pl. 378, no. 5; 1968, pl. 376, nos. 4–5); *Poros-Katsambas* (Wilson and Day 2000, 53; Wilson, Day, and Dimopoulou-Rethemiotaki 2004, 69); *Pyrgos Cave* (Xanthoudides 1918a, 156–159); *Sendones* (Hope Simpson 1995, 373; Betancourt 1996, 380–381); *Sivas* (Watrous and Hadzi-Vallianou 2004, 540); *Stravomytis Cave*, near Archanes (Platon 1950, 532; Sakellarakis and Sapouna-Sakellaraki 1997, 378); *Trapeza* (Watrous and Hadzi-Vallianou 2004, 540); *Vryses Kydonias Cave* (Kera Speliotissa) (Tzedakis 1967, 506); *Ziros Siteias* (Alexiou 1965, 552).

Figure 5.16. A chalice from the Pyrgos Cave illustrates the zonal decoration favored by some potters, HM 7489 (after Betancourt 1985, 28, fig. 16). Scale 1:5.

Figure 5.17. Chalice from the Pyrgos Cave with a scalloped rim, HM 7487 (photograph by Chip Vincent). Ht. 20.5 cm.

the nearby offshore islands begin before Troy I, which makes them earlier than when the shape begins in Crete, indicating that the influences have to travel from north to south. The shape most likely reached Crete by way of the Cyclades, and Cycladic examples of the chalice circulated in Crete along with the locally made pieces (see discussion on p. 74).

The decoration of the chalices was varied and creative. Horizontal incised lines were often used to enhance its shape, and some vases used more than one zone of the burnished patterns (Fig. 5.16). The burnished lines could be vertical, horizontal, or diagonal, and unburnished areas were often left plain to provide contrast with the burnished parts. The form of the chalice was also variable, with conical or rounded shapes for the bowl, or even with a crinkled rim that seems to make a series of different places from which to drink (Fig. 5.17).

Like the chalice shape itself, burnished decoration has many parallels outside Crete. Enhancing pottery this way is a very wide-spread practice in this part of the world (lists of sites are given by several authors: French 1961, 114 n. 38; Fischer 1967; Hennessy 1967, 40; Sperling 1976, 316 n. 7; Betancourt 1985, 28–29). The parallels do not have much meaning in reconstructing specific lines of diffusion, because the notion of polishing a vase is a very simple one that was surely often carried along with the general dissemination of the concept of pottery making, and it could also have been independently invented many times.

Several other shapes were also manufactured in the Dark Gray Burnished Class. One popular form was the ring-footed bowl, also called a chalice with low base (Fig. 5.18). The shape is between 10 and 20 cm high, making it a little large for a cup intended for just one person, and like the chalice, it may be a communal drinking vessel. It often had two handles, which would have facilitated passing it from person to person within a group.

The Fine Dark Gray Burnished Class was a popular tradition. Although early examples were low-fired, the potters soon learned to take advantage of the new kiln technology to create hard and durable vessels while keeping the dark colors that had a long and popular earlier tradition in Crete. A large number of shapes were made in the style (Figs. 5.19, 5.20). Some of them were open and designed for serving and drinking, while others were intended to hold small amounts of food or other items. Many of these vases were given rounded bases.

A bottle is illustrated in Figure 5.21. It has panels of cross-hatched burnished lines separated by groups of vertical lines. The vase has a flat base and decoration only on the upper shoulder, which is the part of the bottle that is most easily seen when the vase sits on a table or some other flat surface below the viewer's eye level. Apparently by the time this bottle was made, the practice of only suspending the vases was abandoned in favor of setting them down.

Figure 5.18. A ring-footed bowl (chalice with low base) from Hagia Photia Siteias, Tomb 200, HNM 3576 (photograph by Chronis Papanikolopoulos). Ht. 13.8 cm.

The finest vases in this style are the biconical pyxides (Fig. 5.22). Like the bottle, these examples come from Hagia Photia, from the end of EM I. Their design is extremely delicate, with thin, hard walls and an interesting shape consisting of a biconical pyxis on tiny legs with a lid that fits down over the upper part of the vase. Burnished designs on the one surviving lid include a star-like design on the upper surface.

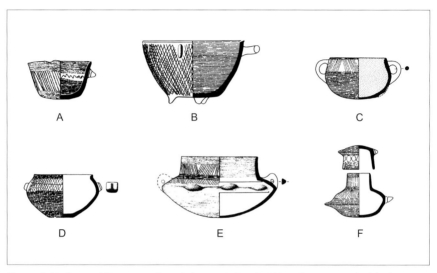

Figure 5.19. Pyrgos Ware vases from Lebena. A. Bowl, HM 15,315. B. Bowl with three feet and a small handle, HM 15,390. C. Two-handled cup, HM 15,364. D. Globular pyxis, HM 15,964. E. Collared jar, HM 15,462. F. Pyxis with cylindrical lid, HM 15,316 (jar) and HM 15,316 (lid) (drawings by Elizabeth Warren, inked by Susan Grice, after Warren 2004, fig. 18, no. 7 [a], fig. 18, no. 10 [b], fig. 19, nos. 27 [c] and 32 [d], fig. 24, no. 240 [e], and fig. 25, nos. 171 and 244 [f]). Scale 1:6.

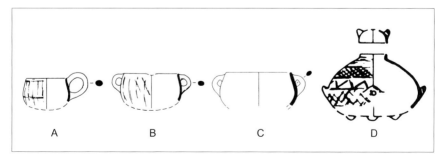

Figure 5.20. Cups and pyxis in the Fine Dark Burnished Class. A. Cup from Knossos (after Hood 1990a, 372, fig. 1, no. 4). B. Two-handled cup from Knossos (after Hood 1990a, 372, fig. 1, no. 5). C. Two-handled cup from Kalo Chorio (after Haggis 1996, fig. 29, no. KT 84). D. Pyxis from Knossos (after Hood 1990a, fig. 2, nos. 14 and 15). Scale 1:6.

Figure 5.21. Pyrgos Style bottle from Hagia Photia Siteias, Tomb 209, HNM 4204 (photograph by Chronis Papaniko-lopoulos). Ht. 10.6 cm.

Figure 5.22. Biconical pyxides from Hagia Photia Siteias, Tomb 2, HNM 2474 (left) and HNM 2506 (right; photographs by Chronis Papanikolopoulos). Ht. 10.6 cm (left) and 14.4 cm (right, including the lid).

THE SCORED STYLE

A series of vessels whose surface is covered with shallow scratches may be called the Scored Style (also called Scored Ware, Wiped Ware, and Brushed Ware). It is most popular in West Crete. The surface treatment, mostly used for jugs and bowls, involves wiping the surface with the ends of a bunch of straws or with a stiff brush (Fig. 5.23). The resulting decoration covers the surface with parallel scratches. The vases are very distinctive, and the effect makes the style easy to recognize. Sometimes the scratches are applied in patterns, so that parallel diagonally or vertically scratched sections can complement one another.

The jugs have raised spouts, indicating the same relationship to gourds as the other examples of this shape. The shape of the bodies is rounded, with rounded or flat bases.

The surfaces of this ware are often dark, and they are evidently fired in an enclosed space, without much oxygen. This is one of the conservative types of pottery that continues from the Neolithic into the Early Bronze Age. The chronology is best attested at Knossos. The Scored Style begins there in the Late Neolithic or Final Neolithic (J.D. Evans 1964, 225), and it continues until EM I (Hood 1961–1962, 93). The long history of the ware mirrors the lengthy life of the Coarse Dark Burnished Class, but all of the jugs with spouts come from EM I.

Sites with the Scored Style

Debla (Warren and Tzedhakis 1974, 321–323, pls. 52d, 53); *Gavdos* (Kopaka and Papadaki 2006, fig. 1, no. 4); *Knossos* (J.D. Evans 1964, 225; Hood 1961–1962, 93; Wilson and Day 2000, 39–41); *Lentaka Cave* at Melidoni Apokoronou (Faure 1965, 57); *Lera Cave* (Davaras 1967, pl. 368, no. 2, upper left); *Mochlos* (Seager 1912, 92); *Phaistos* (Levi 1976, pl. 9b); *Platyvola Cave* (Alexiou 1964, pl. 523a); *Poros-Katsambas* (Wilson and Day 2000, 53; Wilson, Day, and Dimopoulou-Rethemiotaki 2004, 69); *Stravomytes Cave*, near Archanes (Sakellarakis and Sapouna-Sakellaraki 1997, 377).

Figure 5.23. Scored Style jug from the Platyvola Cave (after Betancourt 1985, pl. 2J). Restored ht. ca. 30–40 cm.

RED TO BROWN MONOCHROME CLASS

Many EM I vases were either left plain or were given a uniform coat of slip applied to their exterior. Not to add decorative embellishment to a vase is a conscious decision. It implies a rather different attitude toward the vessel from the impetus to add a design: the form itself is sufficient to make the vessel desirable enough to be used in the manner intended. Undecorated vessels form a large part of the EM I inventory.

The Monochrome Class was popular throughout Crete, especially for medium-sized closed vessels (ca. 20–30 cm tall). In East Crete many potters made their vases with the Calcite-Tempered Fabric Group that had been developed for the Coarse Dark Burnished Class, creating a different appearance only by firing the vases in a kiln chamber instead of in a closed environment. Different local fabrics were used in other parts of the island. Sometimes the workshops that used the new kilns turned out products that were red to brown instead of dark gray. With the higher temperatures creating better ceramics, many potters abandoned the time-consuming burnishing, even though they continued to use many of the traditional steps in clay selection, addition of temper, and manufacturing techniques. The resulting vessels, mostly jars, differed greatly in general details. They could be smoothed, wiped with the hand, or even burnished, and many examples made of tempered clay were covered with a fine-textured slip to improve the surface (and help with the retention of liquid contents). Many members of this class were fired in kilns to create red to brown surface colors.

The monochrome group is rather disparate. It includes the highly burnished red vases called Salame Ware by Branigan (1970b, 18), but some members of the class were wiped but not really burnished at all. At

Knossos, colors of surface slips varied from red to reddish brown to brown, a few vases were burnished lightly before the application of the surface slip, and the fabric itself also varied considerably in color (Wilson and Day 2000, 39). The choice to omit any patterns or designs was common across the entire island, even with vases that were made in new EM I shapes and fired in the newly introduced kilns.

Open shapes were made in many different styles, including the monochrome class. The open bowls in Figure 5.24 come from Knossos. A conical drinking vessel with horns on its rim near the handle is from Nea Roumata in West Crete (Fig. 5.25). The horns would go out of fashion in EM I, but the practical shape of the cup with a vertical handle would become even more common in later centuries.

Many small EM I pyxides can be placed in the monochrome class. A small box from Hagia Photia in eastern Crete (Fig. 5.26) is a small jar or pyxis with a conical lid that fits down over the collar. It is a common shape that is unusual only in that this example has a long cylindrical spout added on the shoulder. One wonders if it was intended as a feeding bottle for a small child. From the small offshore island of Gavdos off the Cretan southwest shore at the other end of the landmass, another pyxis with a somewhat related shape is also monochrome (Fig. 5.27). No lid was found, but one must have been intended. Pyxides come in many different designs. A

Figure 5.24. Open bowls with rounded bases from Knossos, with a red burnished surface. The restored handles are uncertain (after Hood 1990a, fig. 1, nos. 8, 9). Scale 1:8.

cylindrical example from Nea Roumata has pairs of pierced lugs designed to either attach the lid or allow the vase to be hung from a peg or rafter (Fig. 5.28).

One of the most interesting shapes made in the Red to Brown Monochrome Class is a closed vase with a lid with vertical horn-like handles on the shoulder (Fig. 5.29). The appendages on the shoulders are sometimes solid, but they are more useful when, as on this vase, they are pierced so they can allow the vase to hang from a cord. This example is covered with red-firing slip and carefully smoothed to create a beautiful, slightly lustrous surface. Its cylindrical lid fits down over the neck. The vase, which could be called a large pyxis, comes from Lebena. It was found on the floor of Tomb II, and it has been suggested that it may have been placed there with other EM I vases as a special offering at the founding of the great tomb (Warren 2004, 192).

Larger storage and serving vessels were also popular. An example of an amphora comes from Gavdos (Fig. 5.30). The shape was inherited from the Neolithic, but this specimen has the thin handles typical of EM I. A jug from Debla, a small site in West Crete (Warren and Tzedhakis 1974), has a cylindrical neck between the globular body and the vase's small mouth

Figure 5.25. Conical cup with horns on the rim from Nea Roumata, Chania P 5376 (photograph courtesy of Yannis Tzedakis and Maria Andreadaki-Vlazaki). Ht. 11.2 cm.

Figure 5.26. Monochrome pyxis with a long spout and two vertically pierced lugs, covered with its cylindrical lid, from Hagia Photia Siteias, Tomb 179, HNM 3837 (photograph by Chronis Papanikolopoulos). Ht. 8.2 cm.

Figure 5.27. Pyxis from Gavdos, Chania P 9605 (photograph courtesy of Yannis Tzedakis and Maria Andreadaki-Vlazaki). Ht. 10 cm.

Figure 5.28. Cylindrical pyxis from Nea Roumata, Chania P 5375 (photograph courtesy of Yannis Tzedakis and Maria Andreadaki-Vlazaki). Ht. 13.2 cm.

Figure 5.29. Red-slipped monochrome pyxis with horn-like
handles on both the shoulder
and lid, from Lebena, Tomb II,
HM 15,306. Ht., including the
handles, 14.3 cm.

Figure 5.30. Amphora from
Gavdos, Chania P 9604 (photograph courtesy of Yannis Tzedakis
and Maria Andreadaki-Vlazaki).
Ht. 18 cm.

(Fig. 5.31). Its spout, a new idea in Crete during EM I, shows that a knowledge of EM I ceramic design existed even in the smaller settlements.

The Cooking Class

One important group of monochrome vases was used for cooking.
Tripod cooking pots and shallow dishes with very thin walls, the two
shapes that would be the most popular Cretan cooking vessels for the next
2,000 years, are both present by Early Minoan I. The use in cooking has
been confirmed by organic residue analysis (J. Evans 2008, 131–135). At
this period, however, they were by no means used universally, and some
sites continued to prepare food in pots that belong to the Coarse Dark

Figure 5.31. Jug from Debla, Chania P 3368 (photograph courtesy of Yannis Tzedakis and Maria Andreadaki-Vlazaki). Ht. 20.5 cm.

Burnished Class. The deep pots supported on three legs may have been introduced from Anatolia (Shank 2005, 105, pl. 11f). The vases were popular there as well, and the shapes seem related. If so, they probably arrived in Crete along with the many other Anatolian traits that can be recognized at this time.

Both the shallow dishes and the tripod vessels were made of red-firing clay. The use of an extra amount of terra rossa in the fabric recipe must have been regarded as a beneficial trait in pottery designed to withstand heat. The red sediment contains a large amount of inert material that will not shrink much (in comparison with the marl clays), and vases with a larger percentage of terra rossa are also coarser and more porous than the fabrics used for other shapes. The resulting fabrics had a low calcareous content because of the lower percentage of marl clay, and they fired to a redder color than the mixtures with less terra rossa.

The tripod vessel in Figure 5.32 is from the EM I cemetery at Hagia Photia. Its stout legs and deep shape will have supported the vase over a fire, and its large size would have provided a substantial amount of food.

The other cooking shape, the cooking dish or baking plate, is shown in Figure 5.33. This example comes from Knossos, from a well filled with EM I pottery (Hood 1990a, fig. 1, no. 10). The thin walls of this shape suggest it was probably left in place over the coals and not moved much.

These two shapes, along with a smaller number of other cooking vases including jars without legs, tripod trays, and a few other vessels, served for much of the food preparation for the rest of the Bronze Age (Betancourt 1980; Martlew 1988; Filippa-Touchais 2000). The limited assortment of vase forms must mean that soups and stews were particularly popular, and that the shallow dishes served for preparing most other recipes.

Figure 5.32. Tripod cooking pot from Hagia Photia Siteias, Tomb 17, HNM 5059 (photograph by Chronis Papanikolopoulos). Ht. 31 cm.

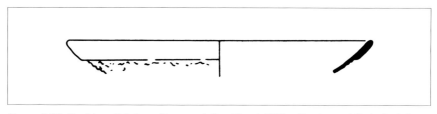

Figure 5.33. Cooking dish from Knossos (after Hood 1990a, fig. 1, no. 10). Scale 1:6.

The Cycladic Styles

Alongside the many classes of pottery that were native to Crete, vases in Cycladic styles also circulated on the island. Unlike the Minoan style vases, whose production either developed in Crete or was modified on the island, the Cycladic style vases stand apart because their entire production is foreign. It has been suggested that some of these vases were manufactured on Crete (Day, Joyner, and Relaki 2003, 19), but they are still Cycladic because their forms, styles, clay recipes, and technologies were entirely dependent on the Cycladic ways of making pottery. Although they had a limited circulation, mostly along the northern coast, they were highly influential in the later Minoan development, and they represent additional choices that were available to the Early Minoan I potters and customers. Large groups of Cycladic style vases come from Hagia Photia Siteias (Davaras and Betancourt 2004), Gournes (Galanaki 2006), Poros-Katsambas (Wilson and Day 2000, 53), and the Pyrgos Cave (Xanthoudides 1918a). In all cases, vessels that were purely Cretan came from the same assemblages.

Most of these Cycladic style vases used a calcite-tempered fabric. Firing for some classes was accomplished in kilns with substantial free oxygen to produce red surfaces, while other products were fired in completely enclosed environments to produce solid gray fabrics with dark exterior surfaces. The Cycladic style pottery mirrors the vases with exclusively Cretan style in that the products all had very complex distribution patterns. Individual sites clearly had multiple opportunities for their supplies of containers.

Chronologically, many of the Cycladic style vases do not come at the very beginning of EM I. At Hagia Photia, some of the graves with these vases also include pottery like the Fine Gray Style that continues to be made in EM IIA. The affinities of the vase shapes in the Cyclades are with the Kampos Group, an assemblage that is not the earliest class in the Aegean islands either. The relative dating for the Kampos Group has been discussed by a long history of scholars, who all conclude that it lies either at the end of EC I or at the opening phase of EC II (see p. 7).

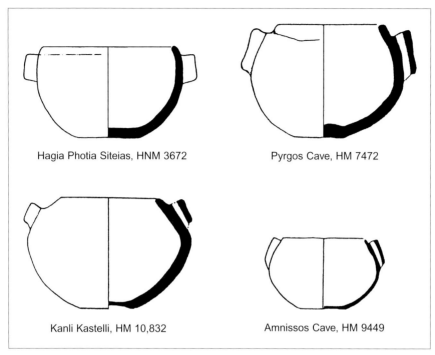

Figure 5.34. Cycladic style globular pyxides from various sites on Crete (modified after Betancourt 2003, 6, fig. 2). Scale 1:3.

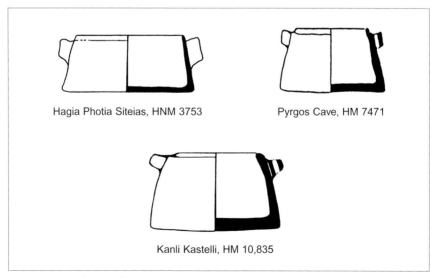

Figure 5.35. Cycladic style conical pyxides from sites on Crete (modified after Betancourt 2003, 5, fig. 1). Scale 1:3.

Among the vases with Cycladic style are a series of pyxides with conical and globular shapes (Figs. 5.34, 5.35). These vases always have carefully fitted dome-shaped lids with pierced lugs on both rim and lid to tie the cover on firmly (Fig. 5.36). They are regularly covered with an attractive red-firing slip. Variations attach more than one vase together to form a group, and the potter sometimes adds a conical base to make the shape more elegant (Fig. 5.37). The conical and globular varieties are obviously made in a similar way, and one supposes they held different varieties of the same product. They all use a clay recipe in the Calcite-Tempered Fabric Group.

A similar way of potting and firing is used for some other shapes. The Cycladic type of chalice is easily recognized by its rounded bulge at the junction between bowl and base (Fig. 5.38). Its shape if often more shallow than the Cretan version, and the different firing technology (i.e., the reducing atmosphere that always made the Cretan class dark) gives the two versions a very different look, but they do not seem to have been differentiated in their uses: at Hagia Photia the two variations were used in exactly the same ways, both as offerings inside a grave and to offer a final toast to the deceased.

The jar with triangular cut-outs shown in Figure 5.39 belongs to the same class of red-slipped vases as the pyxides and chalices. Most of these

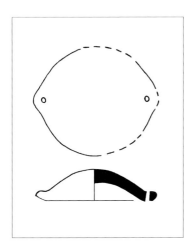

Figure 5.36. Cycladic style lid for either a globular or a conical pyxis, from Pseira (after Betancourt and Davaras, eds., 2002, 126, ill. 19). Scale 1:2.

Figure 5.37. Cycladic style kernos composed of three conical pyxides supported on a conical base, with a single lid covering all three containers, from Hagia Photia Siteias, Tomb 203, HNM 3895 (photograph by Chronis Papanikolopoulos). Ht. 9 cm.

Figure 5.38. Cycladic style chalice from Hagia Photia Siteias, Tomb 166, HNM 4939 (photograph by Chronis Papanikolopoulos). Ht. 29 cm.

Figure 5.39. Jar with cut-outs from Hagia Photia Siteias, Tomb 85, HNM 3970 (photograph by Chronis Papanikolopoulos). Ht. 20 cm.

interesting vessels come from tombs found in the Cyclades (members of the class are collected by Doumas and Angelopoulou 1997, 550, fig. 12). None of the jars from Hagia Photia have any signs of burning inside them, and the original purpose is obscure, though a use as lanterns or incense burners is the most likely possibility.

Other Cycladic shapes have a very different style of manufacture, decoration, and firing, suggesting a different set of production centers that are based on totally separate traditions. One of the most popular shapes in this group is the bottle (Fig. 5.40). The most common variety has a globular body and a conical neck with a restricted mouth and a small outturned rim. The shape, sometimes called Pelos Ware after a cemetery on Melos where it was first found (Betancourt 1985, 32), is associated with the Kampos Group in the Cyclades (Renfrew 1972, pl. 5, nos. 3–6). It is well designed to hold liquids that would be tightly closed with a stopper. Decoration, usually composed of large chevrons, is incised into the clay, and the vases are fired in a completely enclosed environment like a pit. The class was popular at several sites, and over a hundred examples were buried with the dead at Hagia Photia (Davaras and Betancourt 2004). A rare variation is modified to make it into a bird (Fig. 5.41). The bird-vase is still functional as a bottle. Its appendages—wings, tail, feet, and neck and head—are solid and do not have an effect on the usefulness of the attractive shape.

Another class of Cycladic vases found at Hagia Photia is also fired in a completely reducing atmosphere, but it differs from the bottles in the style

Figure 5.40. Two bottles from Hagia Photia Siteias, Tomb 2, HNM 2513 (left) and HNM 2518 (right; photographs by Chronis Papanikolopoulos). Both 10 cm high.

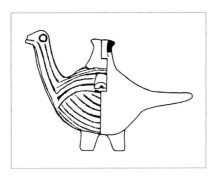

Figure 5.41. Cycladic style bottle modified to create the image of a bird, Hagia Photia Siteias, Tomb 216, HNM 4890 (courtesy of the Hagia Photia Project, Temple University). Scale 1:6.

of its incised decoration. Several different shapes can be grouped together by their firing technology and similar style of ornament. A large group consists of open bowls with straight or slightly rounded profiles and tab handles. The handles, which rise from the rim or are attached on the bowl's exterior all the way from rim to base (Figs. 5.42, 5.43), have endless variations: rounded, square, rectangular, pierced with one hole, pierced with two holes, or plain. The shape probably originates in the northeast Aegean where examples with a similar shape have been found (Hood 1981–1982, I, fig. 40, nos. 251 and 254 [Hagio Gala, Chios], and fig. 106, nos. 9–12, pl. 57, below [Emporio, Chios]).

The decoration is applied to a bowl's exterior, and it consists of a rather limited set of incised designs (Fig. 5.43). It is this restricted inventory of designs that allows the bowl with tab handle to be related to another interesting shape, the frying pan (Figs. 5.44, 5.45). This enigmatic vessel is well known from Cycladic examples. It has a long later history in the Keros-Syros Group, the main assemblage of EC II in the Cycladic Islands

Figure 5.42. Bowl with tab handle from Hagia Photia Siteias, Tomb 122, HNM 3954 (photograph by Chronis Papanikolopoulos). Ht. 6.5 cm.

Figure 5.43. Underside of bowl with tab handle from Hagia Photia Siteias, Tomb 1, HNM 2501 (photograph by Chronis Papanikolopoulos). Ht. 4.4 cm, width with handle 24.0 cm.

Figure 5.44. Frying pan as seen from the side, from Hagia Photia Siteias, Tomb 89, HNM 2627 (photograph by Chronis Papanikolopoulos). Ht. 4.2 cm.

Figure 5.45. Underside of a decorated frying pan from Hagia Photia Siteias, Tomb 71, HNM 2674 (photograph by Chronis Papanikolopoulos). Ht. 4.3 cm.

Figure 5.46. Spool pyxis from Hagia Photia Siteias, Tomb 2, HNM 2510, with lid HNM 2491 (photograph by Chronis Papanikolopoulos). Ht. 2.8 cm.

(Coleman 1985). The purpose of the frying pan has been controversial, and the shape has been regarded as a drum (Mylonas 1959, 125), a bowl (Mylonas 1959, 125–126; Coleman 1985, 203), a mirror (Mellink 1956, 53), a symbolic representation of a female figure (Zschietzschmann 1935), and a bowl for divination (Goodison 2006, 377). The close relationship between these decorated examples suggests that its history begins as a bowl decorated on the bottom, even if it assumes other symbolism later.

Several pyxides can also be joined to this group by their use of the same technology and ornament. The pieces include some attractive examples. Among the designs that repeat a motif found on the bowls are the example on a pyxis shown in Figure 5.46. The base and the top of the cylindrical lid extend beyond the diameter of the small cylindrical box, giving the piece a spool-like appearance. Incised lines decorate the top and sides.

The Cycladic pottery industry was very influential in Crete during the Early Bronze Age. Several EM I vases have Cycladic counterparts, and some of them, like the chalice, were among the most important of the Minoan shapes. The most important conclusion that can be drawn from the presence of these products, however, does not stem from any one shape, but from the total picture. EM I was a complex ceramic period when dozens of different kinds of pottery circulated within the island. The stimulating interchange of ideas would have contributed to advances in every aspect of the industry, and it would have helped make Minoan ceramics a very creative movement.

Decoration with Raised Moldings: The Pithoi

Although pithoi are known from several EM I sites in Crete, the only examples that are complete enough to understand the shape come from Aphrodite's Kephali. The EM I date for this class of vessel is also established by the presence of the large vases at Knossos in a well containing EM I pottery (Wilson and Day 2000, 48–50), at Debla (Warren and Tzedhakis 1974, 323), and at Kalo Chorio, a site also inhabited in EM I (Haggis 1996, 674, fig. 30, no. KT 87).

The tradition of making pithoi was extremely important because it facilitated the large-scale storage of perishable goods. The advantage of containers that would hold up to 165 kilos of goods that could not be ruined by rodents, insects, and mold is that it provided a means for bulk storage that would otherwise not be available. The Cretan vases were fired in kilns, so the tradition was not present in the island until after the arrival of this technological improvement in EM I.

A minimum of nine examples of the pithos come from Aphrodite's Kephali (four examples are shown in Figs. 5.47–5.50). The vases were all designed with the same general shape, consisting of a large rounded body and a vertical collar. Four vertical handles were placed on the shoulder, but they would have been more useful in tying the vases down during transport or in sliding or rolling them about on the ground rather than in lifting them if they were full, because even a well-fitted handle would probably break off with any attempt to lift a full container of this size. The most complete

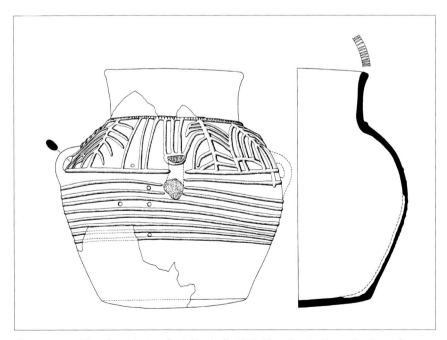

Figure 5.47. Pithos from Aphrodite's Kephali, AK 9 (drawing by Doug Faulmann). Ht. 74.6 cm.

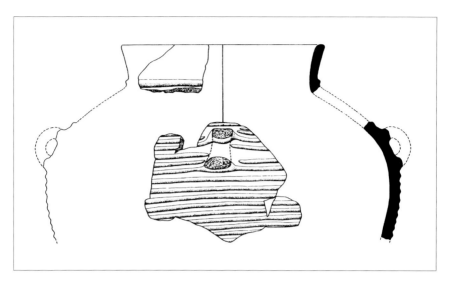

Figure 5.48. The upper part of a pithos from Aphrodite's Kephali, AK 113 (drawing by Doug Faulmann). Dia. of rim 54 cm.

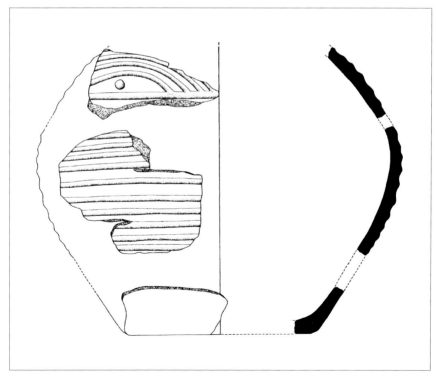

Figure 5.49. Part of the lower two thirds of a pithos from Aphrodite's Kephali, AK 111 (drawing by Doug Faulmann). Dia. of base ca. 42 cm.

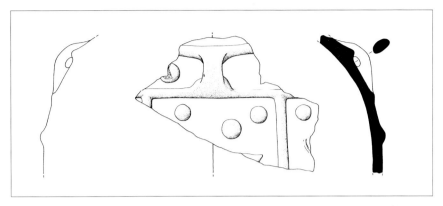

Figure 5.50. Part of the shoulder of a pithos from Aphrodite's Kephali, AK 110 (drawing by Doug Faulmann). Dia. of body ca. 78–80 cm.

vessel (Frontispiece, Fig. 5.47) had a rounded base, suggesting the large jars were usually tipped and then rolled when they needed to be moved as an alternative to trying to lift such a heavy item, but at least one example (Fig. 5.49) had a flat base.

The examples from Aphrodite's Kephali were made from the fabric with red angular inclusions. The potters used a rather coarse variety of this fabric and then finished the vases by smoothing the exterior, adding decoration of raised moldings, and then painting the vessels with a fine-textured slip to make them more impervious to water. The moldings had a structural purpose in addition to the obvious ornamental one. Moldings strengthen the wall without making it thicker, which helps support the vase during drying, and they are also an advantage during firing because thick walls are more likely to break. In addition, the moldings do not add as much weight as a thicker wall.

Such large vessels would have required a large firing chamber. Modern traditional potters build their kilns on the side of a hill so that they can access the firebox from the lower part of the hill and the chamber for the vases from the uphill side, but we have no evidence at all for how Bronze Age pithoi would have been fired except for the information from the vases themselves. Because the fabric is pale colored and the slip is red, we can see that kilns that were large enough for such vases did exist. In fact, they would have been essential for such large shapes because of the difficulties of firing such large objects evenly with any other system (raising the temperature quickly or unevenly causes differential expansion that breaks the object being fired).

In addition to the difficulties in making and firing such large vessels, their transport would also have posed new problems. Movement by ship was probably preferred for long-distance transport. Human beings could have carried the vases if they were fitted onto slings on horizontal poles to be carried by four individuals, or pack animals could have been used. Oxen were available in Crete as early as Early Neolithic. The date of the first arrival of the donkey in Crete is not known, but the animal, originally a desert dweller in North Africa, was already domesticated in Egypt by Predynastic to Early Dynastic times (Partridge 1996, 95).

The decoration of the pithoi was achieved with the raised moldings. The vase in Figure 5.47 has horizontal moldings added on the body, panels of herringbone and vertical moldings on the shoulder, and a horizontal molding setting off the plain collar. The top of the straight rim is enhanced with a row of incisions. The shoulder decoration is not bilaterally symmetrical, and the surviving side has two vertical herringbone motifs on one side of the handle and only one on the other.

From differences in the diameters of rims, bodies, and other parts and from variations in the fabric and the decoration, the many pithos sherds from Aphrodite's Kephali can be sorted into groups. A minimum of nine pithoi are represented. The example in Figure 5.48 has closely spaced raised bands added to the body. The pithos in Figure 5.49 has widely spaced horizontal moldings on the body, and rising stacked crescents grace the shoulder. The vase in Figure 5.50 uses a series of rectilinear boxes with raised dots within them. All the decorations that survive seem to be different from one another, and perhaps each large vase was given its own unique decoration. This system would have been useful in remembering what each vase contained, which would prevent the necessity of looking inside several vases when a portion of a specific commodity needed to be removed.

The general shape of these vases, a form called a collared jar, suggests that they are inspired by pithoi made in the Cyclades. Many variations of the collared jar exist among the vases in the Cycladic style from Hagia Photia (Fig. 5.51). They all consist of a rounded body to which a conical or cylindrical collar is added. If the vase is to be closed, it can either receive a stopper inside a constricted mouth (Fig. 5.51B, C), or the lid can be manufactured so that it fits over the top. We know that pithoi were already known in the Cyclades during the Final Neolithic period, because sherds have been found, even if no complete examples can be reconstructed (Cycladic examples come from Ftelia on Mykonos [Sampson 2002, 81–82, figs. 76–78; 2006, 178]; Tharrounia on Kastri [Sampson 1993], Kastria, Kalavryta [Sampson 1997], and Saliagos on Antiparos [Evans and Renfrew 1968, figs. 42, 43]). The pithoi from Aphrodite's Kephali are actually only large versions of the collared jars, and the example shown in Figure 5.51A bears a close resemblance to the pithos shape except for the size. Even the large vertical herringbone design that decorates the pithos in Figure 5.47 has a parallel in Cycladic ornament (Fig. 5.51C). In spite of these parallels, however, the fabric of the pithoi is a common East Cretan clay recipe, and the large containers were surely manufactured on the island where they were used.

A more distant origin for the shape has also been suggested (Koehl 2008). The Ghassulian culture of the Golan region in the southern Levant used several different shapes of pithoi, including some examples that arc generally similar to those from Aphrodite's Kephali (Epstein 1998, pl. 5, nos. 2, 4, pl. 6, nos. 1, 2, 4). It is not impossible that this part of the East Mediterranean had a role in the Aegean at this time, but some of the other aspects of the eastern culture have no EM I parallels, and the Cyclades provide a geographically closer explanation for the transmission of the pithos shape to Crete.

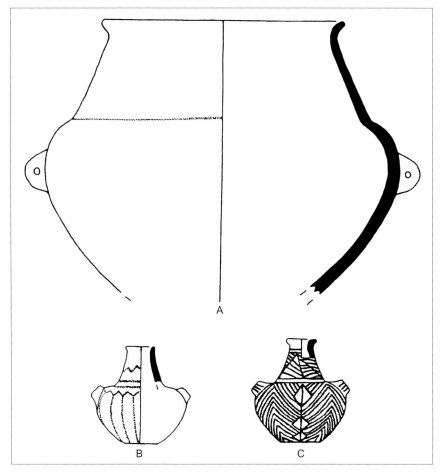

Figure 5.51. Cycladic style versions of the collared jar from Hagia Photeia Siteias. A. Collared jar, HN 3136, Tomb 111. B. Bottle, HN 2946, Tomb 62. C. Bottle, HN 3477, Tomb 19 (courtesy of the Hagia Photia Project, Temple University). Scale 1:3.

6

Comments and Conclusions on the Pottery

The radical changes that occurred in Cretan ceramic manufacture at the beginning of the Bronze Age were a positive force in the history of the island. It is surprising that it took so long for sophisticated kilns to arrive in Crete, considering that they had been used elsewhere in the eastern Mediterranean for some time. When the improved pyrotechnology finally did reach the southern Aegean, it did not spread across the island all at once. In fact, in some villages it would be several years before the taste for dark colored and heavily burnished pottery was abandoned completely in favor of the newer styles.

The Ceramics Revolution

In its mature form, the innovations that are first seen in EM I Crete represent a total technology. The new ways of making ceramics included a series of successive steps from selection of raw materials to distribution of the final products. The stages are summarized below.

SELECTION OF RAW MATERIALS

Final Neolithic potters in Crete preferred coarse clays because such materials are well suited to firing conditions that are less than optimal. Uneven temperatures in fires and pits create thermal shocks that can crack or break thin ceramics, and the temperature in such firings can rise so quickly that only coarse pottery can withstand the rapid escape of water vapor and other gases. The unpredictable nature of Neolithic pyrotechnology forced the potters to use fabrics that were extremely tolerant of rapid and uneven changes in temperature.

With better kilns, the EM I potters could more successfully control both the range of temperatures within the chamber and the speed with which the amount of heat increased. Because of these improvements, they could now choose either fine or coarse clays and be more confident their products would be successful. They were not limited to the coarser clay varieties, and they could collect materials that better suited the intended use of the final product. The most easily visible result was an increased use of the fine-grained, highly calcareous marl clays that were exploited for the finer classes of ceramics.

CLAY PREPARATION

In their mixing of clays, the EM I potters were able to more clearly match their recipe to the finished product. Both pale colored marine clay and red terra rossa were mixed together in different amounts. For fine vases intended for display and serving, the potters added a large amount of the calcareous marine clays that could be refined to eliminate most of the coarser stones. The refining process, called levigation, was accomplished by pounding the clay lumps to reduce them to powder and then putting the clay in water to allow the coarser grains to sink to the bottom so the finer clay could be collected for use. The high calcium content of the marl clays made the final product pale colored and smooth, and the calcite's fluxing action resulted in more highly vitrified vases that were harder and more durable than their predecessors. More terra rossa was added for cooking vessels, resulting in a non-calcareous red fabric that would not break when set over a fire. Large vessels needed to be thicker so they would not slump before they dried, so coarse clays with added temper were used for them. Many fabrics were employed during the period, indicating a great range of decisions in clay preparation.

THE SHAPES

Neolithic potters mostly made cups, bowls, and jars. The inventory of shapes was expanded greatly in EM I, drawing on inspiration from gourds, sea urchins, bags, and even small animals. Vessels were increasingly designed for specific purposes. The vases for transport and serving of liquids now used jugs with elevated spouts that could pour the contents in a directed stream to avoid spilling. In addition, the elevated spouts would not drip. The cylindrical necks of EM I jugs could be tightly sealed with plugs for shipping, and when the vase reached its destination, its spout converted it into a serving vessel. Small items that were not liquid enough to pour were put in pyxides with open mouths and tightly fitting lids that could be tied with string for shipping. Tripod legs lifted the cooking pots above the fire, while frying or baking was accomplished in shallow dishes. Cups, tankards, goblets, and chalices provided for either communal or individual drinking. Specialty shapes, including a few vases shaped like little animals, added an interesting note for ceremonies.

DECORATION

Because they were dark colored, Neolithic vases were not well suited for painted decoration, and most ornament from this period consisted of modifying the surface by adding incisions or burnishing or scoring. The highly calcareous fabrics used during EM I were pale rather than dark because of their high calcium content (see Ch. 3), so paint contrasted nicely. If the body of the vase was not pale enough, the potters simply painted it with a lighter slip. Because the vessels had to be recognized to market the commodities they contained, the EM I potters experimented with a whole series of ornamental systems. Burnishing, incising, scoring, painting in red on a white surface, and painting in white on a red surface were all employed during this period.

THE PYROTECHNOLOGY

The sophisticated kilns were one of the most important factors in the new technology. The separation between firebox for fuel and firing chamber for vessels meant that the potter now had absolute control over temperatures and atmospheric conditions in the kiln by the simple methods of adding or not adding fuel and keeping the doors and the chimney open or partly open or closed. With this new control, the potters were now able to increase the range of their products.

DISTRIBUTION OF THE FINAL PRODUCT

The dissemination of the EM I vases was apparently restricted almost entirely to Crete. The extensive trade networks that developed to distribute the pottery were dynamic and complex, and they were probably constantly changing. Pottery was sent to places where it was not manufactured both for itself and for the goods it contained. The feed-back to the makers of the pottery from this distribution outside the immediate vicinity of the workshops cannot be minimized. It is surely responsible for the rapid development of decorative schemes to suit particular classes of pottery as well as for the repetition of those schemes after a specific product became associated with its visual appearance. Such visual "labels" are a common world-wide phenomenon in all societies that market commodities in containers, especially if the packaging conceals the nature of the product.

The new technological expertise encouraged a new period of experimentation in ceramics. The potters adapted what they saw from elsewhere, copying vessels in other materials and ceramics about which they learned from imports or from their own travel, and they also invented new forms themselves. As a result, EM I included a very wide range of styles, with many classes of vessel. The ceramics industry experienced a real revolution, and the changes were so pronounced that modern historians use them to mark the artificial line between the Neolithic period and the Early Bronze Age.

That these changes were gradual and did not affect all locations in Crete at the same time or in the same ways does not change their radical nature. The ceramic innovations played a crucial role in facilitating transport and storage, and they helped improve the domestic economy of every household that used them. They allowed bulk storage in large amounts, creating a new form of wealth that released a few segments of the population from the necessity of spending most of their time in subsistence farming. They facilitated transport by sea, opening up possibilities for exchange in other goods and services as well. Their decorations encouraged creative movements in the expression of ideas in symbolic ways, and their use in ceremonies emphasized visual focal points for human emotions. All of these movements were important in various ways, and they can be seen as individual steps on the path toward advancement in Cretan society.

Two examples can help explain the visual adjustments that were made to clay vases to make them function both as useful containers and as aesthetic objects whose appearance went beyond what was necessary to fulfill their utilitarian roles. Figure 6.1 illustrates the bird-shaped vase from Hagia Photia, as seen from above. The basic form is the ordinary bottle, complete with its small lugs to allow it to be hung for storage. Additions of head and tail (both solid) increase the resemblance to a bird, and the incised lines on the bottle are extended to the new appendages. The adjustments turn the vase into a fanciful image that still functions as a bottle but has an added appeal as an interesting and amusing new creation. The

Figure 6.1. Bird-shaped bottle photographed from above, Hagia Photia Siteias, Tomb 216, HNM 4890 (photographed by Chronis Papanikolopoulos). Ht. 15.3 cm.

spouted jug in Figure 6.2 is very different. It is enhanced by adding painted ornament. The decoration is conceived as a three-dimensional organization that takes note of the shape. The painted designs divide the form bilaterally at the spout to give it two identical halves, and the use of different designs on spout, shoulder, body, and handle acknowledge the shape of the vessel.

These two vases illustrate different philosophies of ceramic decoration. In both cases, the original form is an ordinary vessel. For the bottle, the potter molds the clay, adds more clay, and incises into its surface to achieve the aesthetic goals. The individual who decorated the jug, on the other hand, does not make any adjustment to the spouted container itself. Aside from the qualities inherent in the original form, this vase relies on a painted pattern applied as a skin over the outer surface. In both cases, the work results in both a utilitarian and an aesthetic function. This dual aspect of ceramic manufacture would continue to be an important characteristic of Minoan pottery.

Figure 6.2. Hagios Onouphrios Style jug from Hagia Photia Siteias, Tomb 202, HNM 4335 (photographed by Chronis Papanikolopoulos). Ht. 25.4 cm.

Part II

7

The Transformation
of Cretan Society

The many years encompassed by the Final Neolithic and Early Minoan I periods were a time of gradual change on the island of Crete. During these centuries, the evidence for what we call the Minoan cultural assemblage gradually emerged. Deep-seated changes in society affected both the ways people lived and the attitudes they adopted toward themselves and their place in the world. The new methods of manufacturing ceramics, which were based partly on influences from overseas and partly from internal needs and inventions, seem to have played one of the pivotal roles in the historical development.

The Case for New Colonists in Crete in FN–EM I

Many scholars have recognized that a large amount of evidence indicates an influx of new residents on Crete between FN and the beginning of EM IIA (among others, see Hutchinson 1962, 140; Branigan 1970a, 11; 1988a, 66; Renfrew 1972, 229; Warren 1973; Tzedakis 1984, 5; Hood 1990a; 1990b). The evidence includes the foundation of new settlements, growth in size of older sites, and many new types of artifacts with no local antecedents. The large number of new sites that have been recorded leaves no doubts about the magnitude of the immigration. New settlements have been recorded in West Crete (Warren and Tzedhakis 1974, 338; Moody

1987, 292–294; Nixon, Moody, and Rackham 1988, 171), Central Crete (Vagnetti 1972–1973; 1973; 1996; Vagnetti and Belli 1978; Vasilakis 1987; Tomlinson 1995, 64; Watrous and Hadzi-Vallianou 2004, 221–226; Panagiotakis 2004; 2006, 169), and East Crete (Betancourt 1999; Branigan 1999a; 2000; Hayden 2003a; 2003b; 2004; Nowicki 1999; 2000; 2002a; 2002b; 2004; 2006; Schlager 2001a; 2001b; Watrous et al. 2000, 474).

The large size of the immigration and its spread over several centuries help prove that the population influx happened, but the complex nature of the evidence caused by the interaction both with those already living in Crete and among the newcomers themselves as well as the changes that occurred after the new colonists arrived in Crete obscure many of the foreign parallels that might have given clues to precise homeland locations. For the pottery, some of the shapes point toward Anatolia (Warren 1973; 2004, 62–63, 72, 113–114, 195; Warren and Hankey 1989, 14; Hood 1990a; 1990b), others suggest the Levant, or Egypt (Weinberg 1965, 307), or the Dodecanese (Nowicki 2002b, 36; 2008, 74), and the Cyclades account for new ideas as well (Davaras 1971; Doumas 1976; Sakellarakis 1976; Broodbank 2000; Betancourt 2003). All of these regions and others probably played at least some role in the increased number of people.

Fragility of New Colonies

Much of the immigration to Crete seems to have occurred during EM I rather than Final Neolithic. Data on new foundations is mostly available from surface surveys. For the Mirabello Bay area, Watrous and his team identified 3 sites with FN pottery and 25 EM I sites (Watrous et al. 2000, 474). Nine Final Neolithic and 19 EM I sites have been recorded for the plain of Phaistos (Watrous and Hadzi-Vallianou 2004, 222–227). These numbers represent a substantial increase. They suggest the relatively rapid arrival of many people after an initial period with only slight habitation.

No matter how well organized or how large a movement of people from one region to another may be, the disruption is bound to create challenges and tensions. Houses have to be constructed, land has to be cleared, crops need to be planted and tended, food and shelter must be arranged for animals, and the new population must deal in some manner with those who were already present. These problems will certainly have existed in a move by sea to the island of Crete.

The large island was already sparsely settled by the end of the Late Neolithic in the fourth millennium B.C. The easy way in which its population increased, however, suggests that the older population was not yet large enough to maintain a monopoly on all of the available land. The new people were able to settle in many parts of their new homeland.

Competition and negotiation for land can take many forms, both peaceful and hostile. Regional differences in the resistance offered by older population elements or by other recent immigrants can be inferred by indirect evidence. Occasional dangers are suggested by the necessity for FN and EM I high and defensible site locations, some of them with fortifications, particularly along Crete's southern and eastern shores (Nowicki 1999; 2000; 2002b, with a catalog of many sites; Schlager 2001a; 2001b). Many of the settlements along the north coast were undefended, suggesting friendly relations with the Cycladic people.

For a society whose people must depend on what is raised on farms, gathered in the wild, or managed as livestock, a migration must have required some adjustments in the new locality. These problems will have been of several kinds. Water resources and skills in water management were important considerations in some regions, but less so in others. The site locations indicate some different strategies. Most of the evidence suggests the new populations were interested primarily in farming and in small-scale herding, but the choice of harbor sites for some communities proves that seafaring could be an important consideration as well. These differences show up in the archaeological record. At Poros, the seaport for Knossos, for example, a substantial amount of the EM I pottery is in Cycladic styles, suggesting overseas relations of some type (Wilson and Day 2000, 53), while the contemporary pottery from Knossos itself is missing this component (Hood 1990a). These contrasts will have resulted in differential access to certain types of commodities, especially those derived from overseas.

In agriculture, harvests in new locations have to wait for the plants to mature. Even under ideal conditions, food must be available for a period of time after land is cleared and planted before anything can be ready to consume. In addition, crops do not always thrive if planted in new soils, and experiments may be necessary to better understand the situation based on planting times, climate, soil conditions, weather, insects, and other local problems.

Livestock has its own issues. Flocks and herds of sheep and goats have to be large in order to provide enough meat to sustain even a single family, and models suggest a time lag before a small group of animals can be large enough to be useful as a substantial food supply. Even if a ewe has a lamb every year, about half of the animals will be male, so the flock does not double its size immediately. A model by Redding (1989) supposed an original stock of 20 ewes with ages between 2 and 3 years. Using modern figures of management and assuming no local predators, a flock would double in size after 8 years and again double after 11 years, so that a generation (ca. 20–25 years) would pass before it would have over 100 sheep, which is large enough to slaughter an animal every week and still maintain the flock at the same approximate level. Another model (Ducos 2000), using slightly different data, calculated that if an immigrant family brings 10 sheep to a new location, the family must wait about the same amount of time before it can slaughter one animal per week to sustain itself with meat. These models begin with flocks or herds of mature animals, but it may not be realistic to assume that adult sheep or goats would be transported on EM I ships, and younger, smaller, and more docile animals may be a more likely hypothesis. In any case, a new colony needs time before it is independent.

The conclusion is obvious. Alternate sources of food must be available for new colonies to supplement what is brought or raised in the new landscape, at least for enough time for the new colony to be able to sustain itself with its own resources. These alternate sources of food can include marine resources, wild plants and animals, re-supply from overseas, or acquisitions from others living already in the new land.

The key to this supply of additional resources is storage and transportability. Livestock and food supplies do not move by themselves. Harvests must come from a location that produces more than is required locally. The crops must be processed in some way for them to be portable, a means of transport must be arranged, and some type of negotiation for the movement of goods must be agreed upon. It is at this point that the necessity for containers arises. Ceramics provide an important component in this necessary support system.

The Storage and Transport of Goods in EM I Crete

It cannot be a coincidence that the massive immigration to Crete happened at about the same time that a development called the secondary products revolution reached the island. The secondary products revolution was an increased use of processed agricultural and animal products (Sherratt 1981; 1983). Several advances in stockbreeding, agriculture, and technology occurred in the Aegean toward the end of the Neolithic. The convergence and interplay between these factors and the ways that they encouraged one another and changed the societies that adopted them would help contribute to the social and economic advances visible in Early Minoan I.

The difference between a primary product and a secondary product is the amount of processing necessary to create the final commodity. Harvested cereals are primary products, while breads and cakes preserved in honey are secondary. Olives are primary, but perfume made from olive oil is secondary. Meats and hides are primary products, while leather, woven fabrics, and dried and salted meats are secondary. Grapes are primary, but the wines made from them can be classified with the processed commodities. In most cases, the secondary products are less subject to spoilage than the primary ones.

The issue is not that secondary products began to be used in EM I, but that the new containers encouraged an intensification in the manufacture, storage, and distribution of both primary and secondary agricultural commodities to a degree that went beyond mere subsistence. The new items that were less subject to spoilage played an important role in the new situation. Many different factors contributed to the availability of these new products.

One advance that made woven fabrics more successful took place in stockbreeding. The difference between hair and wool is that the latter has small hook-like appendages that allow it to be spun more satisfactorily to make thread, while the former does not. The wild ancestor of the species of domestic sheep that was raised in Crete had hair, not wool. At some time during the latter part of the Neolithic, sheep that had wool were bred somewhere in Europe or Asia, and the breed reached Crete. Spindle whorls and loom weights are present at Final Neolithic sites in Crete, including Knossos (J.D. Evans 1964, 233, 235, fig. 56) and Nerokourou (Vagnetti, Christopoulou, and Tzedakis 1989, 73–74). They suggest the presence of spinning and weaving, though the exact date when the warp-weighted loom appeared remains uncertain. The new woolen fabrics stimulated the production of textiles (Barber 1991, 20–29; 1992, 101), and Crete's mountainous landscape was ideally suited to the pasturage of sheep.

Wool has several advantages over flax and other ancient fibers. It can be used to weave cloth that is warmer than clothing of the same weight made of other fibers, and thick woolen fabrics are almost waterproof. By matting the fibers instead of weaving them, felt is produced, which is even more waterproof, and it can be made into very useful shapes for people who spend much of their life out of doors, like hats and capes. Wool also takes many kinds of organic dyes much more easily than flax, and multicolored threads facilitate the making of complex designs. The advantages of colored designs in the production of elite fabrics would have been immediate, making fine cloth an important item of exchange and an object of high prestige (Michailidou 2005, 26–29).

Another advance in stockbreeding was the domestication of the donkey. The wild animal was native to northern Africa, so it is assumed that the appearance of domestic donkeys in Pre-Dynastic and Early Dynastic Egypt represents an early stage in their use by man (Partridge 1996, 95). Donkeys are a superior pack animal to oxen because they carry heavy burdens, subsist on poor fodder and little water, and live as long as 40 years. We do not know when the animal reached Crete (Brodie 2008), but its appearance elsewhere in the eastern Mediterranean at this time must have encouraged trade in general, including in regions still depending on oxen.

An advance also took place in olive culture. Although olive wood shows up as charcoal in Cyprus early in the Neolithic period (Thiébault 2003), it does not appear in Crete until much later. Pollen records show that the species (perhaps wild) became more abundant only after 5,000 B.C. (Bottema 1980; Bottema and Sarpaki 2003; Moody, Rackham, and Rapp 1996). By the beginning of the Early Bronze Age, it was available as a fruit as well as for its oil and the products like perfume that could be made from olive oil. Olives are stored in liquids (usually olive oil or vinegar), and the oils and perfumes made as secondary products are also liquids, so they require water-tight containers.

We do not know when the many other secondary agricultural commodities were first used, but organic residue analysis of pottery from the Gerani Cave in West Crete has tentatively identified milk products in a Neolithic ceramic container (Craig 2008). One can assume that milk and at least some of its byproducts were probably available as early as animals were domesticated, if not earlier. Secondary products made from milk include curds, whey, cheeses, yogurt, and butter (Greenfield 1988), but cheese is the item than can be preserved for the longest time. The important point to consider for EM I Crete is that better containers allowed these products to be shipped and stored more successfully.

Many other processed foods are possible. Cakes and bread made from grains can be stored in honey, and fruits also preserve very well in this medium. Fish and meats are kept successfully in brine or salt. Wines, including flavored varieties, have good value as food, and the wine can also be made into vinegar, which is an excellent preservative for foods. All kinds of pickled vegetables, including some wild ones like artichokes, can be kept in vinegar. Other products, like sauces and spiced foods, are also likely.

What all of these products have in common is that they are subject to damage from fungus and microbes and from insects, mice, rats, and other small animals. Moth larvae and several other types of insects will eat woolen cloth. Mice and rats can enter storerooms through soil floors, and they can climb stone walls and chew their way into rooms at ceiling level.

Boxes and bags of leather, cloth, wood, basketry, and other organic materials are all easily damaged, and they have to be checked frequently to insure they are still secure.

In economic terms, the new ceramic technology in Crete was not important for its production of art objects but for the improvement in insect-proof and vermin-proof containers. Neolithic clay vases leaked slowly because they were porous and broke easily because they were fired to low temperatures. As soon as better containers for both the primary and secondary products became available, they stimulated the production of everything that could now be stored, shipped, and traded more easily. Valuable goods could now be accumulated and kept more easily for future use.

The storage of agricultural products resulted in a new form of easily portable wealth. This wealth was acquired through a series of steps. First, land that produced an excess over local needs was required. The harvests from that land, either faunal or agricultural, were processed to make products that could be packaged in medium-sized, easily lifted clay containers. The resulting wealth could then be kept for winter needs, hoarded for the future, distributed to clients, or transported to where the product was in greater demand and exchanged at a profit for something else. Control of these steps, or of any one of them, provided a new form of power.

The system must have altered the economy greatly. For the faunal products, an important economic advance was that the animals were no longer killed if the main product was wool or cheese. The flocks were a sustainable resource that increased in size and kept on producing instead of becoming depleted. The new products created a way to achieve social and political control over essential commodities. Production, taxation, trade, or piracy and warfare could all yield wealth and power.

The new aspects of the economy must have stimulated nascent developments in several areas, because cultures are always characterized by complex linkages with many components. Increased sea trade required more ships plus the crews to man them, and caravans of donkeys or oxen were needed if products moved by land. The raising of sheep would have increased, with flocks kept for wool or cheese instead of meat, and advances in weaving techniques would have followed swiftly. In the archaeological record, we can note the appearance of loom weights signifying the warp-weighted loom (Hoffmann 1974), advances in seafaring (Broodbank 1999, 20–22), and a great increase in trade (Wilson and Day 1994). Hints of an intensification of agriculture have also been noted at this time (Halstead 2000, 117–122). The ceramics industry responded vigorously.

Metallurgy and the Pyrotechnology of EM I Ceramics

No intensification of technological knowledge occurs in isolation. Advances in one area stimulate other new ways of doing things, leading both to new discoveries and to applications of old knowledge in fresh situations. The rapid adoption of new ways of making, decorating, and firing pottery that occurred in Crete in the late 4th to early 3rd millennia B.C. was not an isolated event, but a part of a general advancement in several different technologies. Aspects of these new concepts reinforced one another. It should not be a surprise that advances in achieving higher temperatures in pottery making happened at the same time that metallurgists learned to achieve higher temperatures to melt or smelt copper, or that both events coincided with the intensification of olive culture with its useful secondary product of crushed olive seeds and skins, a much more efficient fuel than wood or charcoal.

It has been suggested that the technology of using high temperatures and reducing atmospheres to smelt copper was first developed for pottery making and then applied to metallurgy (Kaiser, Franklin, and Vitali 1986). The direction of the borrowing of technology remains unclear, but certainly the development of early pottery styles can only be understood within its historical context, and the metalworking that required high temperatures developed at the same time as higher-fired ceramics. More important for the present study is the relative role of the two materials within the EM I culture. New pottery styles and new objects of metal were both innovations at the beginning of the Early Bronze Age in Crete, but the nature of their impact was very different.

Items indicating copper working (slag, crucibles, pieces of copper ore, and fragments of other metallurgical debris) come from several Final Neolithic to Early Minoan I sites on Crete, indicating that the technology of making objects from metal had already reached Crete by this period (Muhly 1996; 2002, 79–80; 2004, 287; Day and Doonan, eds., 2007). Smelting at Chrysokamino begins in Final Neolithic (Muhly 2004; Betancourt 2006), and similar remains suggesting other nearby smelting sites have been reported from Kavousi (Haggis 2005, 109) and Pacheia Ammos (Mosso 1910, 289–292), with all three places in the Gulf of Mirabello region. A copper blade was found at EM I Kalo Chorio (Haggis 1996, 662). Copper and copper slag also comes from the FN to EM I site of Kephala Petras in East Crete near Siteia (Papadatos 2007) and from the EM I settlement and metallurgy workshop at Poros near Knossos (Dimopoulou-Rethemiotaki, Wilson, and Day 2007; Wilson, Day, and Dimopoulou-Rethemiotaki 2008).

The late EM I sites at Gournes (Galanaki 2006) and Hagia Photia (Davaras and Betancourt 2004; Day, Wilson, and Kiriatzi 1998) have a whole series of metal objects from late EM I, and two crucibles come from the latter location (Betancourt and Muhly 2007). Silver was also used in Crete in the Neolithic to Early Minoan I periods (Vasilakis 2008, 75–77).

The copper smelting technology is best understood from Chrysokamino. A reconstruction of the process (Betancourt 2006, fig. 4.1) suggests a simple system. The ore, fuel, and flux are placed in a small cavity in the soil, and a cylindrical chimney over it aids in pulling the draft upward, bringing in air at the base. The workshop was built on a very windy cliff-top location, but additional air would have been a help in the process. By EM III the workshop was using clay bellows to help assure a strong draft, but the same results could have been achieved by using blowpipes, a technique that is well known from Old Kingdon Egyptian tomb paintings (Betancourt 2006, fig. 4.2). The blowpipes would be hollow reeds, and a tuyere (like an example found at Chrysokamino) would keep the end of the pipe from being burned by the furnace. This reconstruction of the smelting technology has been tested experimentally with successful results (Catapotis, Pryce, and Bassiakos 2008).

Smelting of this type would have produced only impure copper that needed to be melted in crucibles so that the impurities would float and purer metal would collect in the bottom of the small clay crucibles. Melting in crucibles probably had a wider distribution than smelting. Like the smelting furnaces, the fires used to melt the copper or silver would have needed either blowpipes or bellows to blow extra air into the fire to make it hot enough to melt the metal; the operation probably occurred within an enclosed space like a small pit furnace excavated into the ground. Two crucibles with copper inside them come from Hagia Photia. Sockets in their bases would have allowed them to be removed from the furnace and tilted to pour the melted copper into a mold. A more complex process is known from Poros where the presence of the arsenic mineral loellingite indicates that the EM I metallurgists were already aware of a way to add arsenic to copper in order to improve the casting. After the casting was made, the final stage would include finishing the object by hammering, burnishing, polishing, and other simple hand processes to complete the object. These Early Minoan techniques have been studied in detail by Thomas Tselios (2008). He found that the earliest artifacts he studied used only simple techniques, consisting of casting followed by hammering or by both annealing and hammering. Annealing is the process of heating an artifact to make it softer and easier to work.

Some of the principles that were behind the metallurgical practices of early Crete were relevant to other technologies from the same period, especially the pyrotechnology needed for the firing of pottery (Kaiser, Franklin, and Vitali 1986). For their kilns and furnaces, both nascent industries needed knowledge of fuels, drafts, insulation to hold the heat within enclosed spaces, and the relationship between time of heating and the resulting effects. Metallurgists made use of clay products, including crucibles that were constructed from fabric recipes that were coarse and porous so they could withstand high heat, so clay sources and the properties of clays and sediments and how these properties could be modified by additions to the fabric were of interest to both groups of Minoan artisans. Most settlements from this period were small enough that one can expect interaction between personnel involved with different activities.

In terms of impact on EM I society, the new copper objects and the new pottery styles offer a striking contrast. Finds of metal objects are extremely rare in EM I contexts, and most sites have yielded none at all. The new classes of EM I pottery, on the other hand, spread more rapidly throughout Crete, and a lively trade carried the vessels to most sites. One must conclude that EM I metal was a rare and sporadically distributed material, while the new pottery classes were much more important culturally and economically.

Growth in Trade

The growth in trade stimulated by the packaging and movement of agricultural products would have brought Crete larger amounts of many other items in addition to foodstuffs, because ancient ships did not specialize in a single cargo. Many of these products came from the north. Obsidian in Crete was mostly from Melos (Cann and Renfrew 1964; Renfrew, Cann, and Dixon 1965; Carter 2008, 225–226). Already in the Neolithic, a few imports of metal objects were being imported into Crete: examples include copper celts from Knossos (Evans 1921–1935, II, 14–15, fig. 3f) and from an unknown context near Ierapetra (Mosso 1910, 309–310, figs. 171, 172) and silver objects from Amnissos (Vasilakis 1996, fig. 69). Metal objects began to arrive in Crete in larger quantities during EM I (Muhly 2002, 79–80; 2004, 287; 2008).

Trade increased by the end of the EM I period. The smelting of imported copper ores discussed in the previous section for the workshop at Chrysokamino (Muhly 2004; Betancourt 2006) and the melting and alloying of copper to make useful artifacts at Poros (Dimopoulou-Rethemiotaki, Wilson, and Day 2007; Wilson, Day, and Dimopoulou-Rethemiotaki 2008) both depended on trade with the north. The same can probably be said for the finds of copper slag that come from Kephala Petras (Papadatos 2007) and the copper that was melted in crucibles at Hagia Photia (Day, Wilson, and Kiriatzi 1998; Davaras and Betancourt 2004; Betancourt and Muhly 2007). Metal objects with Cycladic affinities were buried in tombs at Gournes (Galanaki 2006), and lead isotope analysis indicates that most Minoan copper from the entire Early Bronze Age came from Kythnos, Seriphos, and Lavrion (Gale 1990; Stos-Gale 1993, 122–123; 1998). Trade was responsible for all of these finds.

All of the discoveries of EM I and earlier metals are related to the north in some fashion (Muhly 2008). They indicate a great increase in Cretan relations in this direction. By the latter part of EM I, during the time of the Kampos Group, the interrelations with the Aegean islands were intense enough to support sites like Gournes and Hagia Photia, whose material culture was almost entirely Cycladic even though they were on Cretan soil.

Were these Cycladic sites in Crete intermediaries in some of this trade? In a time before written records, it is easy to see why overseas exchange routes would have required local managers to arrange for storage and shipment of commodities. Especially in a time when new trade was being arranged, local advisors and managers would have facilitated the process greatly.

That these interrelations between Crete and the Aegean islands had an effect on the pottery industry is shown by the northern connections for many of the shapes adopted by Cretan potters. In addition to influences from the Cyclades, the islands must also have been the intermediaries for the many influences from Anatolia, all of which had to pass through their waters in order to reach Crete. Ceramic shapes with northern parallels used in Crete include the chalice, the spherical pyxis, the conical and straight-side pyxides, the barrel vase, the tripod cooking pot, the jug with elevated spout, and all of the Cycladic style vases including the bowl with tab handle, the frying pan, and the collared jar. The pithos tradition that begins in Crete at this time may be especially heavily indebted to Cycladic predecessors. It is likely that a northern connection had a strong influence on kiln technology and many other aspects of the pottery industry.

With new foundations and new and more portable wealth came the need to defend it. Storage of goods in small jars or pithoi was very different from land that could not be moved or grain that was placed in large permanently constructed bins or animals that had to be herded and fed and tended. Jars could be loaded on board a ship and taken away quickly, and their contents were anonymous if they were put in other containers. Clay vessels filled with valuable goods could be stored, given away, exchanged, or buried with the dead for use in the next life. It is not surprising that evidence for fortified sites intensifies at just this period (Branigan 1999a; 1999b; Nowicki 1999; 2002b; 2006; Schlager 2001a; 2001b). Filled storerooms were too valuable to be left undefended.

Social Stratification and Nascent State Formation: The Case of Aphrodite's Kephali

Most of the writers who have examined the evidence for social stratification during the early stages of Early Minoan Crete have reached somewhat negative points of view. Several scholars have approached the problem by looking for expressions of elite status in elaborate personal adornment, rare and skillfully made objects, and monumental architecture, with the assumption that elite members of a social group would use these items to distinguish themselves from those who were not members of the same privileged class. With these assumptions, it is difficult to assume that pronounced stratification existed before the middle of the third millennium B.C. with the appearance of the rich tombs at Mochlos (Soles 1988). Indeed, several writers have suggested that elite members of society in Crete only developed toward the end of the Early Bronze Age and that the island had an egalitarian society in Final Neolithic and EM I (Cherry 1983, 40; Whitelaw 1983, 337–340; Branigan 1995, 39; Sbonias 1999, 28). Are these assumptions necessarily correct? Can we assume that they operated at the beginning of the Bronze Age in a society with no tradition of what we regard as ostentatious display?

The methodological problem with these conclusions is that the argument that leads to them assumes that wealth and power would have been displayed at the beginning of the third millennium B.C. in the same way as it would be a thousand years later. A different conclusion is possible if one first examines the society's specific material culture and judges it based on its own value systems, not on those of a different and much later period. EM I society built on the value systems of the immediately preceding Final Neolithic. The people who lived in Crete during the Final Neolithic had no tradition of monumental tombs or even of moderately large ones. They buried their dead in caves or in tiny cist graves without elaborate burial goods, so we cannot expect to see the presence or absence of stratification from this type of evidence. Even during EM I, this society had very little metal, almost no figural art, and little tradition of elaborate personal adornment. It was a fragile culture, with many settlements still facing the challenges of adjusting to a new homeland or of competing with neighbors who were suddenly more numerous. Prosperity may not have consisted of elaborate personal adornment or of public displays of metal objects or figural art, but of storerooms filled with durable containers containing essential goods that would last until the next harvest. Hunger and famine were not just abstract concepts, and power must have been judged by the control of enough food to allow the community to survive and prosper, and by the protection of that community from potentially hostile forces who might try to acquire what they did not raise themselves.

In examining the archaeological record for evidence of this type of power, one alternative approach to the problem of the recognition of stratification in society is to examine the evidence regionally instead of locally. One can get a very different picture if one examines a society in regional terms instead of by looking only at an isolated individual site. For a settlement like EM II Myrtos, for example, the absence of dramatic differences between the architecture and the artifacts found in different parts of the community leads to the probably correct conclusion that the site did not have an elite ruler living there (Warren 1972, 266–267; Whitelaw 1983, 333–334). However, this conclusion should not be extended to the entire region, because Myrtos itself may not provide any evidence for whether or not its residents owed allegiance to a regional polity centered at some other, more important location. Examining individual tholos tombs in the Mesara can lead to the conclusion that these small sites were egalitarian (Branigan 1995, 39), but what about Phaistos, which was already a much larger site even in FN (Vagnetti 1972–1973)? If one examines the Mesara as a region, a great site at Phaistos and smaller ones situated across the landscape can lead to a conclusion that some type of organization must have existed, a conclusion that is supported by the evidence for the existence of an integrated regional society in the Mesara in both FN and EM I that held ceremonial feasts at Phaistos (Relaki 2004, 176–180).

Complex aspects of society can also be recognized at Knossos. The site was also a large settlement during the Neolithic, and the very early integration of the large center with its surrounding territory can be documented by the fact that about half of the EN–MN pottery used at the site was manufactured elsewhere, all but 10% within a 7–30 km distance from the large settlement (Tomkins 2004, 38). This pattern of consumption changed in LN when an enormous increase occurred in the volume of local ceramics, accompanied by more efficient production and decorative systems, perhaps signifying a change to full-time local craftsmen (Tomkins 2004, 52). With 15% of this larger volume of ceramics still being imported from elsewhere, however, the pattern of importation was still present. The local importation of pottery from as far away as the Mesara continued into EM I (Wilson and Day 1994).

We lack this type of evidence for most other parts of Crete, but hints of emerging complexity exist from other indications. From the Isthmus of Ierapetra, for example, one can examine the evidence for two other indications of social stratification, traces of attempts to achieve regional goals and evidence for large-scale communal storage. A regional goal like the construction of a communal building designed to serve more than one settlement involves either cooperation or management at a greater than local level, with the implication that someone is expressing a degree of management and supervision to achieve those mutual goals. Communal storage beyond the needs of a single family is proof of the collection and maintenance of what, at the beginning of the Bronze Age, must have been considered wealth. For EM I, evidence for both of these situations can be examined from the site of Aphrodite's Kephali.

The Isthmus of Ierapetra is a natural trade route, because it is the only place in Crete with an easy passageway north and south across the mountainous island. Aphrodite's Kephali is a small EM I site overlooking this north–south route (Betancourt 2008). The hilltop is a strategic location because it has a cave entrance (that would have been a good place for storage and possibly a source of water) as well as a good view of the landscape all the way to the south coast 7 km away. The spot is not very hospitable, and it is occasionally buffeted by raging winds even during the summer.

The small site is surrounded by the remains of a fortification wall. Within the wall are the remains of a small two-room building, a courtyard, and a fire area with evidence for large fires. The kephali is a single-period site, with EM I pottery including the Hagios Onouphrios Style in two fabrics, the Coarse Dark Burnished Class, the Monochrome Class, and other vases. Its finds include extensive evidence for storage, including a minimum of nine pithoi.

The most complete pithos holds 165 kilos if filled to the brim. With at least nine of these large containers, the fort stored a minimum of 1,485 kilos of goods, not counting the many other vessels found in the excavations. This storage capacity goes well beyond the needs of a single family, suggesting that this building was a communal storage place for secondary agricultural products. The wall around the site indicates that such a large hoard of food needed protection.

Storage was also present in smaller clay vases. Analysis of the contents of vessels by gas chromatography has shown that both olive oil and wine were stored here. The new evidence is a welcome addition to the archaeological record for this period. It provides information to help correct the absence of data that once existed for the presence of olive oil (Hansen 1988, 44–46, 51–52) and wine (Halstead 1988, 529) at the beginning of the Early Minoan period.

The remarkable thing about Aphrodite's Kephali is that it represents a regional set of objectives involving at least some measure of defense during EM I. The site is too small to be an independent farmstead, and it does not have the animal bones, marine shells, stone tool assemblage, and other artifacts to suggest domestic habitation. With at least nine pithoi, it also has much more storage than one would expect for a tiny habitation site. The walled courtyard and the evidence for signal fires suggest it is either a refuge for local people in times of danger, a guard-post at a boundary, or a small fort to claim and oversee the road in the valley below. For all of these possibilities, the watchtower and its garrison have to have been stocked with supplies and managed in order to achieve aims that go beyond farming the nearby hills.

The large number of pithoi meets the need for a hierarchical intervention in craftwork that has been regarded as one criterion for the emergence of elite control within society (Schoep and Knappett 2004, 27) that reached a peak in the Late Bronze Age (Christakis 2008). The building of a substantial stone construction suggests the same conclusion. The little fort would have involved some serious labor. Large and small blocks were quarried lower on the hill and transported up to the small headland for building. Moving the pithoi there would have been difficult as well. One can assume the site had some symbolic value, because when it was destroyed at some time during EM I, its pithoi were smashed and scattered instead of trying to retrieve them for use elsewhere. The spot was never inhabited again.

The easiest assumption for this site is that it was a cooperative venture for mutual goals. One assumes that lighting the fire would have been a signal to tell others whatever was intended: to run to the fort for refuge, or collect taxes from a caravan on the road, or something else. Whatever the exact explanation, the fort suggests political decisions on a regional level, and this may imply social stratification, or even a nascent small polity overseeing nearby communities.

The situation at the beginning of the Early Bronze Age requires some new questions. If trade in Hagios Onouphrios Style vases was routinely moving across Crete (Wilson and Day 1994), why should we not assume that someone was amassing wealth and power by helping to manage and control some of that trade? If famine was an ever-present danger, would wealth be measured by control of rooms containing pithoi and other clay containers filled with valuable foodstuffs, and would prestige be judged by the ability to provide that food in times of need? Why would someone build a fort and fill it with commodities stored in pithoi, if not to render assistance to those who appreciated the efforts and how the power was used? Given the complex and changing social and economic structure of EM I, the growing reliance on trade and other interactions between communities, and the natural tendency to competition by human beings, why would anyone think that personal power was not sometimes achieved? New questions can lead to some new answers.

Ceramic Containers and Self-Identity

It is difficult to know how much of the high-quality ceramics was a response to the new need for better-quality storage vessels to support the secondary products revolution and how much of the secondary products intensification was, itself, inspired by the fact that the commodities could now be stored and shipped more successfully. The "multiplier effect" discussed in detail by Colin Renfrew (1972, ch. 21) suggests that a series of advances can mutually interact with one another, leading to a progressive development that encourages all of them. A complex interaction between a long series of advancements in technology, transport, food production, elite competition, and many other factors helps explain the resulting development better than any one item in isolation.

Because ceramic containers were one of the key factors in the storage of goods that allowed people to survive from one harvest to the next and also one of the most visible aspects of a trade network that extended to all of Crete, the potters were well aware of their role in the economy of EM I. They responded with creativity and skill. A good example of the attitude of the potters toward their work is illustrated by the pithoi from Aphrodite's Kephali. By examining the fragments closely and noting differences in fabric, surface treatment, and dimensions, a minimum of nine different pithoi can be recognized. No two were exactly alike. The proportions and form were generally similar, but they varied slightly in dimensions, and they were all decorated individually with raised clay moldings. The manufacture of these large jars was not approached as a job of mass production and repetitive actions, but as a creation of individual vessels, each with its own appearance and its own personality. The potters were aware that they were making a product that had not been attempted in Crete before the time of these great jars, and that it required skill both in manufacture and especially in firing. Such large vessels take a long time to make. For the firing, the upper part of the kiln will have been built especially for each firing, and the scale of the chamber will have been much larger than kilns for smaller vases. The pride of accomplishment is visible in the careful decoration of each vessel, and the appreciation also extended to the users: the best surviving example cracked at some time in its history, and it was mended so that it could continue to be used.

The creation of individual and unique clay containers extends to a large number of the workshops of EM I, particularly those making pots with the new EM I technology. The vases of the Hagios Onouphrios Style and the Lebena Style are painted with great skill. Many of them are unique art objects, conceived as small sculptures as well as useful containers. The makers of many of these vases were situated somewhere in the south-central part of Crete, and it is worth noting that the most creative pieces were found near where they were made. The most inventive shapes were acquired, used in life, and then buried with the dead in the communal tombs used by the South Cretan settlements, while those exported to other parts of Crete were more ordinary shapes that were more simply decorated and less creative. The use-patterns speak loudly of self-awareness and a communal identity in which the users of the vessels associated themselves with their own locale and its familiar products to an extent that they wished to be associated with them in death as well as in life.

The arrival of the tholos tomb in Crete represents some of the earliest monumental stone architecture in the island. The circular tomb chambers are most common in South Crete, with only an occasional example else-where in the island (Xanthoudides 1924; Branigan 1970b). This architec-ture, however, is used for a set of communal burial practices that are island wide and that have some characteristics whose antecedents can be traced well back into the Neolithic period. Early Minoan burial practices were communal, with dozens or hundreds of individuals buried in the same tomb. The customs associated with the dead were extremely complex, involving communal activities both at the time of death and on later occasions, with the collection, movement, and re-deposition of the human bones as well as with associated ceremonies involving the consumption of food and drink and various other commemorative activities (Branigan 1987). Burial cere-monies were obviously an important activity within the community.

With this background, the deposition of large amounts of the new EM I ceramics in Minoan tombs must have been an important activity that was charged with symbolic meaning. Elaborate deposition did not occur at every location. It is most apparent in the Mesara, at places like Lebena and Hagia Kyriaki. Unfortunately, the Hagia Kyriaki tomb was so badly looted in modern times that its evidence cannot be studied so easily. Lebena, how-ever, furnishes us with a prime example of the new burial mode (Alexiou and Warren 2004). The deposit of dozens of examples of EM I pottery of the highest quality in some Minoan tombs provides a fine example of the new attitude toward these fine classes of ceramic vessels. They tell us both about the nature of the pottery and about the attitude of the people toward the symbolic meaning of these vessels, which were used to help define their owners in death as well as in life. The volume of clay vases in some of these EM I cemeteries is far greater than in Final Neolithic ones.

The explanation for this new concern for clay vases as burial goods, like many human activities, probably has its roots in many complex factors. Part of the reason may be that EM I society was more affluent than its predecessors: more people were wealthy enough to remove valuable goods from use and deposit them with the deceased. Other aspects, however, must also be involved, because the ability to carry out an activity does not fully explain the motive to actually do it. The qualities of the vases themselves must also be involved.

Some of the most dynamic aspects of many of the new vases involve their visual qualities. The interesting shapes and the bold decorations and bright, slightly lustrous surfaces contrast sharply with the darker Neolithic ceramics. These visual aspects make them suitable as visual focal points for whatever memory they invoke, even if the vase is new and the memory will be the burial service. If the vase was owned by the deceased, it can invoke a memory of life and use.

Another quality is permanence. One of the most important aspects of clay vases in comparison with burial offerings of wood, leather, cloth, and other organic materials is their permanence. Organic materials decay and disappear, losing the qualities that stimulate memory and trigger the remembrance of the person they accompanied. With their custom of moving the bones of the deceased, the Minoans were well aware of these qualities. The increased numbers of vases at tombs like Lebena may be based partly on the permanence they express. Permanence can be a strong symbolic quality in contrast with death. Burial customs assert the continuity of the family and the community in the face of individual deaths. Offerings to the deceased assert the continuity of the surviving members of the community from the past into the future, and visual focal points for these feelings can be important. The new vases, with their strong individual character and their permanence, represented new visual metaphors.

Final Statement

EM I has evidence for large sites like Knossos and Phaistos in sharp contrast with the many smaller places, long-distance trade on a routine basis, large-scale storage of bulk commodities, new forms of display in some tombs but not in others, and the presence of communal architecture with large-scale storage. Only social stratification and the presence of differential amounts of power can explain all of this evidence. A strong case exists for the presence of regional polities at least in some parts of Crete, with important implications for the nature of the emerging Minoan society.

Minoan culture advanced on a path that included both some strong local and regional variations as well as some characteristics that defined the island as a whole. This complex combination of traits can only have developed in an island with frequent contact between regions that still maintained something of their local identity. Travel and long-distance trade, however, require safe passages. The ability to travel freely between mountainous locations or across the sea implies some respect for the safety of the travelers, merchant ships, and traders, which in turn implies a controlling power with the ability to punish brigands and pirates. Only an organized community can put the welfare of the group above the greed of the individual. The evidence suggests that small polities were already in existence during EM I, and that they helped create the safer living conditions.

An important result of the new economic and social situation in EM I must have been increased stability. The fragility of the recent colonies that has been suggested above during their initial periods of establishment was giving way in favor of a more secure situation thanks to the ability to store goods, especially foods, for longer periods of time. The contrast between the insecurity of the Final Neolithic as attested by sites like Katalimata (Nowicki 2008) and the greater confidence of EM I must have led to larger settlements and a more secure way of life. These developments must have contributed to the stability and advancement that would create what we call the Minoan culture.

References

Alexander, B. 1978. "CeramActivities. Terra Sigillata," *Ceramics Monthly* 26 (no. 1, Jan.), pp. 89–93.

Alexiou, S. 1951. "Πρωτομινωϊκαὶ ταφαὶ παρὰ τὸ Κανλὶ Καστέλλι Ἡρακλείου," *KrChron* 5, pp. 275–294.

———. 1964. "Συντήρησις καὶ ἀποκατάστασις μνημείων," *ArchDelt* 19 (Β΄, 3 Chronika), pp. 444–447.

———. 1965. "Ἀρχαιότητες καὶ μνημεῖα Κεντρικῆς καὶ Ἀνατολικῆς Κρήτης," *ArchDelt* 20 (Β΄, 3 Chronika), pp. 549–557.

———. 1967. "Ἀνασκαφαί," *ArchDelt* 22 (Β΄, 2 Chronika), pp. 482–488.

Alexiou, S., and P. Warren. 2004. *The Early Minoan Tombs of Lebena, Southern Crete* (*SIMA* 30), Sävedalen.

Back, M.E., and J.A. Mandarino. 2008. *Fleischer's Glossary of Mineral Species,* Tucson.

Barber, E.J.W. 1991. *Prehistoric Textiles: The Development of Cloth in the Neolithic and Bronze Ages with Special Reference to the Aegean,* Princeton.

———. 1992. *Women's Work, the First 20,000 Years: Women, Cloth and Society in Early Times,* New York and London.

Barber, R.L.N. 1987. *The Cyclades in the Bronze Age,* London.

Barnard, K.A. 2003. "A Macroscopic Analysis of the Neopalatial Fabrics," in *Mochlos* IB: *Period III. Neopalatial Settlement on the Coast: The Artisan's Quarter and the Farmhouse at Chalinomouri. The Neopalatial Pottery*

(*Prehistory Monographs* 8), by K.A. Barnard and T.M. Brogan, Philadelphia, pp. 3–12.

Barrett, J.C., and P. Halstead, eds. 2004. *The Emergence of Civilisation Revisited* (*Sheffield Studies in Aegean Archaeology* 6), Oxford.

Bernabò-Brea, L. 1964–1976. *Poliochni. Città preistorica nell'isola di Lemnos, I–II* (*Monografie della Scuola Archeologica di Atene e delle Missione Italiane in Oriente* 1–2), Rome.

Betancourt, P.P. 1980. *Cooking Vessels from Minoan Kommos: A Preliminary Report,* Los Angeles.

———. 1983. *The Cretan Collection in the University Museum, University of Pennsylvania* vol. I. *Minoan Objects Excavated from Vasilike, Pseira, Sphoungaras, Priniatikos Pyrgos, and Other Sites* (*University Museum Monograph* 47), Philadelphia.

———. 1985. *The History of Minoan Pottery,* Princeton.

———. 1990. *Kommos* II: *The Final Neolothic through Middle Minoan III Pottery,* Princeton.

———. 1995. "Kommos Survey: Selected Artifacts, Minoan Sites: Pottery," in *Kommos* I: *The Kommos Region and Houses of the Minoan Town.* Part I: *The Kommos Region, Ecology, and Minoan Industries,* J.W. Shaw and M.C. Shaw, eds., Princeton, pp. 380–387.

———. 1996. "3. Kommos Survey: Selected Artifacts. Minoan Sites: Pottery," in *Kommos* I: *The Kommos Region and Houses of the Minoan Town,* J.W. Shaw and M.C. Shaw, eds., Princeton, pp. 380–383.

———. 1999. "What is Minoan? FN/EM I in the Gulf of Mirabello Region," in *MELETEMATA: Studies in Aegean Archaeology Presented to Malcolm H. Wiener as He Enters His 65th Year* (*Aegaeum* 20), P.P. Betancourt, V. Karageorghis, R. Laffineur, and W.-D. Niemeier, eds., Liège and Austin, pp. 33–40.

———. 2003. "The Impact of Cycladic Settlers on Early Minoan Crete," *Mediterranean Archaeology and Archaeometry* 3, pp. 3–11.

———. 2006. *The Chrysokamino Metallurgy Workshop and Its Territory* (*Hesperia Suppl.* 36), Princeton.

———. 2008. "Aphrodite's Kephali," *Kentro: The Newsletter of the INSTAP Study Center for East Crete* 11, pp. 12–13.

Betancourt, P.P., L. Berkowitz, and R.L. Zaslow. 1990. "Evidence for Minoan Basket[s] from Kommos, Crete," *Cretan Studies* 2, pp. 73–77.

Betancourt, P.P., and C. Davaras, eds. 2002. *Pseira* VI: *The Pseira Cemetery* 1. *The Surface Survey* (*Prehistory Monographs* 5), Philadelphia.

———. 2003. *Pseira* VII: *The Pseira Cemetery* 2. *Excavation of the Tombs* (*Prehistory Monographs* 6), Philadelphia.

Betancourt, P.P., H.M.C. Dierckx, and D.S. Reese. 2003. "Tomb I: Catalog of Objects" and "Tomb III: Catalog of Objects," in *Pseira* VII: *The Pseira Cemetery 2. Excavation of the Tombs* (*Prehistory Monographs* 6), P.P. Betancourt and C. Davaras, eds., Philadelphia, pp. 7–16, 36–37.

Betancourt, P.P., E. Koss, R.F. Lyon, and S. Montgomery. 1979. "The Techniques of Manufacture," in *Vasilike Ware: An Early Bronze Age Pottery Style in Crete. Results of the Philadelphia Vasilike Ware Project* (*SIMA* 56), by P.P. Betancourt, Göteborg, pp. 12–20.

Betancourt, P.P., and J.D. Muhly. 2007. "The Crucibles from the Aghia Photia Cemetery," in Day and Doonan, eds., 2007, pp. 146–153.

Betancourt, P.P., and G.H. Myer. 1995. "Phyllite Fabrics in Eastern Crete," in *The Ceramics Cultural Heritage. Proceedings of the International Symposium The Ceramics Heritage of the 8th CIMTEC-World Ceramics Congress and Forum on New Materials, Florence, Italy, June 28–July 2, 1994* (*Techna—Monographs in Materials and Society* 2), P. Vincenzini, ed., Faenza, pp. 395–399.

Blackman, D., and K. Branigan. 1978. "Moni Odigitrias Area," *ArchDelt* 27 (Chronika), pp. 630–631.

———. 1982. "Excavation of an Early Minoan Tholos Tomb from Ayia Kyriaki, Ayiofarango, Southern Crete," *BSA* 77, pp. 1–57.

Blegen, C.W., J.L. Caskey, M. Rawson, and J. Sperling. 1950. *Troy: General Introduction. The First and Second Settlements,* Princeton.

Blitzer, H. 1984. "Traditonal Pottery Production in Kentri, Crete: Workshops, Material, Techniques and Trade," in *East Cretan White-on-Dark Ware: Studies on a Handmade Pottery of the Early to Middle Minoan Periods* (*University Museum Monograph* 51), by P.P. Betancourt, Philadelphia, pp. 143–157.

Bonacasa, N. 1967–1968. "Patrikiès–Una stazione medio-minoica fra Haghia Triada e Festòs," *ASAtene*, n.s., 29–30, pp. 7–54.

Bottema, S. 1980. "Palynological Investigations on Crete," *Review of Paleobotany and Palynology* 31, pp. 193–217.

Bottema, S., and A. Sarpaki. 2003. "Environmental Change in Crete: A 9000-Year Record of Holocene Vegetation History and the Effect of the Santorini Eruption," *The Holocene* 13 (5), pp. 733–749.

Branigan, K. 1970a. *The Foundations of Palatial Crete: A Survey of Crete in the Early Bronze Age,* New York and Washington.

———. 1970b. *The Tombs of Mesara,* London.

———. 1987. "Ritual Interference with Human Bones in the Mesara Tholoi," *Aegaeum* 1, pp. 43–50.

———. 1988a. "Some Observations on State Formation in Crete," in French and Wardle, eds., 1988, pp. 63–71.

————. 1988b. *Pre-Palatial: The Foundations of Palatial Crete,* Amsterdam.

————. 1995. "Social Transformation and the Rise of the State in Crete," in *POLITEIA: Society and State in the Aegean Bronze Age (Aegaeum* 12), R. Laffineur and W.-D. Niemeier, eds., Liège and Austin, pp. 33–39.

————. 1999a. "Late Neolithic Colonization of the Uplands of Eastern Crete," in *Neolithic Society in Greece (Sheffield Studies in Aegean Archaeology* 2), P. Halstead, ed., Sheffield, pp. 57–65.

————. 1999b. "The Nature of Warfare in the Southern Aegean," in *POLEMOS: Le context guerrier en Égée à l'âge du bronze (Aegaeum* 19), R. Laffineur, ed., Liège and Austin, pp. 88–93.

————. 2000. "Lamnoni—A Late Neolithic Landscape in Eastern Crete," in *Πεπραγμένα Η΄ Διεθνούς Κρητολογικού Συνεδρίου* A (1), Herakleion, pp. 161–167.

Brodie, N. 2008. "The Donkey: An Appropriate Technology for Early Bronze Age Land Transport and Traction," in Brodie et al., eds., 2008, pp. 299–304.

Brodie, N., J. Doole, G. Gavalas, and C. Renfrew, eds., 2008. *Horizon: A Colloquium on the Prehistory of the Cyclades,* Cambridge, UK.

Broodbank, C. 1999. "Colonisation and Configuration in the Insular Neolithic of the Aegean," in *Neolithic Society in Greece (Sheffield Studies in Aegean Archaeology* 2), P. Halstead, ed., Sheffield, pp. 15–41.

————. 2000. *An Island Archaeology of the Early Cyclades,* Cambridge, UK.

Broodbank, C., and T.F. Strasser. 1991. "Migrant Farmers and the Neolithic Colonization of Crete," *Antiquity* 65, pp. 233–245.

Cann, J.R., and C. Renfrew. 1964. "The Characterization of Obsidian and Its Application to the Mediterranean Region," *Proceedings of the Prehistoric Society* 30, pp. 111–133.

Carter, T. 2008. "The Consumption of Obsidian in the Early Bronze Age Cyclades," in Brodie et al., eds., 2008, pp. 225–235.

Catapotis, M., O. Pryce, and Y. Bassiakos. 2008. "Preliminary Results from an Experimental Study of Perforated Copper-Smelting Shaft Furnaces from Chrysokamino (Eastern Crete)," in *Aegean Metallurgy in the Bronze Age,* I. Tzachili, ed., Athens, pp. 113–121.

Cherry, J.F. 1983. "Evolution, Revolution and the Origins of Complex Society in Minoan Crete," in Krzyszkowska and Nixon, eds., 1983, pp. 33–45.

Christakis, K.S. 2005. *Cretan Bronze Age Pithoi: Traditions and Trends in the Production and Consumption of Storage Containers in Bronze Age Crete (Prehistory Monographs* 18), Philadelphia.

————. 2008. *The Politics of Storage: Storage and Sociopolitical Complexity in Neopalatial Crete (Prehistory Monographs* 25), Philadelphia.

Colburn, C.S. 2008. "Exotica and the Early Minoan Elite: Eastern Imports in Prepalatial Crete," *AJA* 112, pp. 203–224.

Coleman, J.E. 1985. "'Frying Pans' of the Early Bronze Age Aegean," *AJA* 89, pp. 191–219.

Cosmopoulos, M.B. 1991. *The Early Bronze 2 in the Aegean* (*SIMA* 98), Jonsered.

Craig, O. 2008. "Organic Residue Analysis of Ceramics from the Neolithic Cave of Gerani, West Crete," in *Archaeology Meets Science: Biomolecular Investigations in Bronze Age Greece,* Y. Tzedakis, H. Martlew, and M.K. Jones, eds., Oxford, pp. 121–124.

Davaras, C. 1967. "Ἀρχαιότητες καὶ μνημεῖα Δυτικῆς Κρήτης," *ArchDelt* 22 (Chronika), pp. 495–501.

———. 1971. "Πρωτομινωϊκὸν νεκροταφεῖον Ἁγίας Φωτιᾶς Σητείας," *AAA* 4, pp. 392–396.

———. 1976. *Guide to Cretan Antiquities,* Park Ridge, NJ.

———. 2003. *Führer zu den Altertümern Kretas,* Athens.

Davaras, C., and P. Betancourt. 2004. *The Hagia Photia Cemetery* I: *The Tomb Groups and Architecture* (*Prehistory Monographs* 14), Philadelphia.

Day, P.M. 1991. *A Petrographic Approach to Pottery in Neopalatial East Crete,* Ph.D. diss., University of Cambridge, UK.

———. 1997. "Ceramic Exchange between Towns and Outlying Settlements in Neopalatial East Crete," in *The Function of the "Minoan Villa." Proceedings of the Eighth International Symposium at the Swedish Institute at Athens, 6–8 June 1992* (*SkrAth* 4°, 46), R. Hägg, ed., Stockholm, pp. 219–228.

———. 2004. "Marriage and Mobility: Traditions and the Dynamics of the Pottery System in Twentieth Century East Crete," in *Pseira VIII: The Archaeological Survey of Pseira Island,* Part 1 (*Prehistory Monographs* 11), P.P. Betancourt, C. Davaras, and R. Hope Simpson, eds., Philadelphia, pp. 105–142.

Day, P.M., and R.C.P. Doonan, eds. 2007. *Metallurgy in the Early Bronze Age Aegean* (*Sheffield Studies in Aegean Archaeology* 7), Oxford.

Day, P.M., L. Joyner, and M. Relaki. 2003. "A Petrographic Analysis of the Neopalatial Pottery," in *Mochlos IB: Period III. Neopalatial Settlement on the Coast: The Artisan's Quarter and the Farmhouse at Chalinomouri. The Neopalatial Pottery* (*Prehistory Monographs* 8), by K.A. Barnard and T.M. Brogan, Philadelphia, pp. 13–32.

Day, P.M., L. Joyner, E. Kiriatzi, and M. Relaki. 2005. "Petrographic Analysis of Some Final Neolithic–Early Minoan II Pottery from the Kavousi Area," in Haggis, 2005, pp. 177–195.

Day, P.M., M. Relaki, and E.W. Faber. 2006. "Pottery Making and Social Reproduction in the Bronze Age Mesara," in *Pottery and Society: The Impact of*

Recent Studies in Minoan Pottery, M.H. Wiener, J.L. Warner, J. Polonsky, and E.E. Hayes, eds., Boston, pp. 21–71.

Day, P.M., D.E. Wilson, and E. Kiriatzi. 1997. "Reassessing Specialization in Prepalatial Cretan Ceramic Production," in ΤΕΧΝΗ: *Craftsmen, Craftswomen and Craftsmanship in the Aegean Bronze Age* (*Aegaeum* 16), R. Laffineur and P.P. Betancourt, eds., Liège and Austin, pp. 275–289.

―――. 1998. "Pots, Labels and People: Burying Ethnicity in the Cemetery at Aghia Photia, Siteias," in *Cemetery and Society in the Aegean Bronze Age* (*Sheffield Studies in Aegean Archaeology* 1), K. Branigan, ed., Sheffield, pp. 133–149.

Dierckx, H.M.C., and B. Tsikouras, 2007. "Petrographic Characterization of Rocks from the Mirabello Bay Region, Crete, and Its Application to Minoan Archaeology: The Provenance of Stone Implements from Minoan Sites," *Bulletin of the Geological Society of Greece* 40. *Proceedings of the 11th International Congress, Athens, May, 2007,* Athens, pp. 1768–1779.

Dimopoulou-Rethemiotaki, N., D.E. Wilson, and P.M. Day. 2007. "The Earlier Prepalatial Settlement of Poros-Katsambas: Craft Production and Exchange at the Harbour Town of Knossos," in Day and Doonan, eds., 2007, pp. 84–97.

Doumas, Ch. 1976. "Prehistoric Cycladic Settlers in Crete," *AAA* 9, pp. 69–79.

―――. 1977. *Early Bronze Age Burial Habits in the Cyclades* (*SIMA* 48), Göteborg.

Doumas, Ch., and A. Angelopoulou. 1997. "Οι βασικοί κεραμικοί τύποι της Πολιόχνης και η διάδοσή τους στο Αιγαίο κατά την Πρώιμη Εποχή του Χαλκού," in *Η Πολιόχνη και η Πρώιμη Εποχή του Χαλκού στο Βόρειο Αιγαίο,* Ch. Doumas and V. La Rosa, eds., Athens, pp. 543–555.

Ducos, P. 2000. "The Introduction of Animals by Man in Cyprus: An Alternative to the Noah's Ark Model," in *Archaeozoology of the Near East IV* (*ARC-Publicatie* 32), Gröningen, pp. 74–82.

Epstein, C. 1998. *The Chalcolithic Culture of the Golan* (*IAA Reports* 4), Jerusalem.

Evans, A.J. 1895. *Cretan Pictographes and Prae-Phoenician Script, with an Account of a Sepulchral Deposit at Hagios Onouphrios,* London.

―――. 1903–1904. "The Palace of Knossos," *BSA* 10, pp. 1–62.

―――. 1921–1935. *The Palace of Minos at Knossos* I–IV, London.

Evans, J. 2008. "Organic Residues in Pottery of the Bronze Age in Greece," in *Archaeology Meets Science: Biomolecular Investigations in Bronze Age Greece,* Y. Tzedakis, H. Martlew, and M.K. Jones, eds., Oxford, pp. 125–143.

Evans, J.D. 1964. "Excavations in the Neolithic Settlement at Knossos, 1957–60," *BSA* 59, pp. 132–240.

Evans, J.D., and C. Renfrew. 1968. *Excavations at Saliagos near Antiparos,* Oxford.

Evely, R.D.G. 2000. *Minoan Crafts: Tools and Techniques. An Introduction,* vol. II (*SIMA* 92 [2]), Jonsered.

Fassoulas, C.G. 2001. "The Tectonic Development of a Neogene Basin at the Leading Edge of the Active European Margin: The Herakleion Basin, Crete, Greece," *Journal of Geodynamics* 31, pp. 29–70.

Faure, P. 1965. "Recherches sur le peuplement des montagnes de Crète: Sites, cavernes et cultes," *BCH* 89, pp. 27–63.

Filippa-Touchais, A. 2000. "Η Τριποδικά Χύτρα στον Αιγαιακό Χώρο κατά τη Μέση Χαλκοκρατία Διάδοση και Σημασία," in *Πεπραγμένα Η΄ Διεθνούς Κρητολογικού Συνεδρίου,* A (3), Herakleion, pp. 421–436.

Fischer, F. 1967. "Ägäische Politurmusterware," *IstMitt* 17, pp. 22–33.

French, D.H. 1961. "Late Chalcolithic Pottery in North-West Turkey and the Aegean," *AnatSt* 11, pp. 99–141.

French, E.B., and K.A. Wardle, eds. 1988. *Problems in Greek Prehistory. Papers Presented at the Centenary Conference of the British School of Archaeology at Athens, Manchester, April 1986,* Bristol.

Galanaki, K. 2006. "Πρωτομινωικό ταφικό σύνολο στην πρώην Αμερικανική βάση Γουρνών Πεδιάδος," in *Πεπραγμένα Θ΄ Διεθνούς Κρητολογικού Συνεδρίου* A (2), Herakleion, pp. 227–241.

Gale, N.H. 1990. "The Provenance of Metals for Early Bronze Age Crete—Local or Cycladic," in *Πεπραγμένα του ΣΤ΄ Διεθνούς Κρητολογικού Συνεδρίου* A (1), Chania, pp. 299–316.

Goodison, L. 2006. "Divination with Water: A Diachronic Perspective," in *Πεπραγμένα Θ΄ Διεθνούς Κρητολογικού Συνεδρίου* A (2), Herakleion, pp. 369–383.

Goren, Y., and A. Gopher. 1995. "The Beginnings of Pottery Production in the Southern Levant: A Model," in *The Ceramics Cultural Heritage. Proceedings of the International Symposium The Ceramics Heritage of the 8th CIMTEC-World Ceramics Congress and Forum on New Materials, Florence, Italy, June 28–July 2, 1994* (*Techna—Monographs in Materials and Society* 2), P. Vincenzini, ed., Faenza, pp. 21–28.

Gosser, G., and S. Sapareto. 1984. "Reconstruction of Potting Techniques and Pyrotechnology," in *East Cretan White-on-Dark Ware: Studies on a Handmade Pottery of the Early to Middle Minoan Periods* (*University Museum Monograph* 51), by P.P. Betancourt, Philadelphia, pp. 126–129.

Greenfield, H.J. 1988. "The Origins of Milk and Wool Production in the Old World," *Current Anthropology* 29, pp. 573–593.

Haggis, D.C. 1996. "Excavations at Kalo Khorio, East Crete," *AJA* 100, pp. 645–681.

———. 2005. *Kavousi I: The Archaeological Survey of the Kavousi Region* (*Prehistory Monographs* 16), Philadelphia.

Haggis, D.C., and M.S. Mook. 1993. "The Kavousi Coarse Wares: A Bronze Age Chronology for Survey in the Mirabello Area, East Crete," *AJA* 97, pp. 265–293.

Halstead, P. 1988. "On Redistribution and the Origin of Minoan-Mycenaean Palatial Economies," in French and Wardle, eds., 1988, pp. 519–529.

———. 2000. "Land Use in Post-Glacial Greece: Cultural Causes and Environmental Effects," in *Landscape and Land Use in Postglacial Greece* (*Sheffield Studies in Aegean Archaeology* 3), P. Halstead and C. Frederick, eds., Sheffield, pp. 110–128.

Hampe, R., and A. Winter. 1962. *Bei Töpfern und Töpferinnen in Kreta, Messenien und Zypern,* Mainz am Rhein.

Hansen, J.M. 1988. "Agriculture in the Prehistoric Aegean: Data versus Speculation," *AJA* 92, pp. 39–52.

Hawes, H.B., B.E. Williams, R.B. Seager, and E.H. Hall. 1908. *Gournia, Vasiliki and Other Prehistoric Sites on the Isthmus of Hierapetra, Crete,* Philadelphia.

Hayden, B.J. 2003a. "Final Neolithic–Early Minoan I–IIA Settlement in the Vrokastro Area, Eastern Crete," *AJA* 107, pp. 363–412.

———. 2003b. "The Final Neolithic–Early Minoan I/IIA Settlement History of the Vrokastro Area, Mirabello, Eastern Crete," *Mediterranean Archaeology and Archaeometry* 3, pp. 31–44.

———. 2004. *Reports on the Vrokastro Area, Eastern Crete* 2: *The Settlement History of the Vrokastro Area and Related Studies* (*University Museum Monograph* 119), Philadelphia.

Hazzidakis, J. 1912–1913. "An Early Minoan Sacred Cave at Arkalochori in Crete," *BSA* 19, pp. 35–47.

Heimann, R.B. 1982. "Firing Technologies and their Possible Assessment by Modern Analytical Methods," in *Archaeological Ceramics,* J.S. Olin and A.D. Franklin, eds., Washington, D.C., pp. 89–96.

Hennessy, J.B. 1967. *The Foreign Relations of Palestine during the Early Bronze Age,* London.

Hess, J., and I. Perlman. 1974. "Mössbauer Spectra of Iron in Ceramics and their Relation to Pottery Colors," *Archaeometry* 16, pp. 137–152.

Hoffmann, M. 1974. *The Warp-Weighted Loom,* Oslo.

Hood, M.S.F. 1961–1962. "Stratigraphic Excavations at Knossos, 1957–1961," *KrChron* 15–16, pt. 1, pp. 92–98.

———. 1966. "The Early and Middle Minoan Periods at Knossos," *BICS* 13, pp. 110–111.

———. 1971. *The Minoans: Crete in the Bronze Age,* London.

———. 1981–1982. *Excavations in Chios 1938–1955* I–II, London.

———. 1990a. "Autochthons or Settlers? Evidence for Immigration at the Beginning of the Early Bronze Age in Crete," in *Πεπραγμένα του ΣΤ´ Διεθνούς Κρητολογικού Συνεδρίου* A (1), Chania, pp. 367–375.

———. 1990b. "Settlers in Crete c. 3000 B.C.," *Cretan Studies* 2, pp. 151–158.

———. 2006. "Mackenzie and the Late Neolithic/Early Minoan I Interface at Knossos," in Πεπραγμένα Θ΄ Διεθνούς Κρητολογικού Συνεδρίου Α (2), Herakleion, pp. 9–21.

Hope Simpson, R. 1995. "The Archaeological Survey of the Kommos Area," in *Kommos* I: *The Kommos Region and Houses of the Minoan Town.* Part I: *The Kommos Region, Ecology, and Minoan Industries,* J.W. Shaw and M.C. Shaw, eds., Princeton, pp. 325–402.

Hurlbut, C.S., and C. Klein. 1977. *Manual of Mineralogy,* New York, Chichester, Brisbane, Toronto, and Singapore.

Hutchinson, R.W. 1962. *Prehistoric Crete,* Harmondsworth.

Jones, R.E. 1986. *Greek and Cypriot Pottery: A Review of Scientific Studies* (*Fitch Laboratory Occasional Paper* 1), Athens.

Karantzali, E. 1996. *Le Bronze Ancien dans les Cyclades et en Crète: Les relations entre les deux régions, influence de la Grèce continentale* (*BAR-IS* 631), Oxford.

Kaiser, T., U.M. Franklin, and V. Vitali. 1986. "Pyrotechnology and Pottery in the Late Neolithic of the Balkans," in *Proceedings of the 24th International Archaeometry Symposium,* J.S. Olin and M.J. Blackman, eds., Washington, D.C., pp. 85–94.

Koehl, R. 2008. "The Role of Ghassulian Culture in the Development of Early Bronze Age Crete," unpublished oral presentation at the conference "The Minoan World: Exploring the Land of the Labyrinth," Alexander S. Onassis Public Benefit Foundation (USA), Inc., New York, Sept. 13, 2008.

Kopaka, K., and Ch. Papadaki. 2006. "Προϊστορική κεραμική από την επιφανειακή έρευνα στη Γαύδο," in Πεπραγμένα Θ΄ Διεθνούς Κρητολογικού Συνεδρίου Α (1), Herakleion, pp. 63–78.

Krzyszkowska, O., and L. Nixon, eds. 1983. *Minoan Society. Proceedings of the Cambridge Colloquium 1981,* Bristol.

La Rosa, V. 1988. "Αγία Τριάδα," *Kretiki Estia* 2, pp. 331–332.

Lamb, W. 1932. "Schliemann's Prehistoric Sites in the Troad," *PZ* 23, pp. 111–131.

———. 1936. *Excavations at Thermi in Lesbos,* Cambridge, UK.

Laviosa, C. 1972–1973. "L'abitato prepalaziale di Haghia Triada," *ASAtene,* n.s., 34–35, pp. 503–513.

Lawrence, W.G. 1972. *Ceramic Science for the Potter,* Radnor, PA.

Leontidis, A. 1996. "Αγγειοπλαστικά κέντρα και περιοδεύοντες τεχνίτες. Η περίπτωση των Μαργαριτών Μυλοποτάμου Ρεθύμνης," in *Κεραμικά εργαστήρια στην Κρήτη από την αρχαιότητα ως σήμερα,* E. Gavrilaki, ed., Rethymnon, pp. 69–77.

Levi, D. 1961–1962. "Gli scavi a Festòs negli anni 1958–60," *ASAtene,* n.s., 23–24, pp. 377–504.

————. 1964. *The Recent Excavations at Phaistos,* Lund.

————. 1965. "La varietà della primitiva ceramica cretese," in *Studi in onore di Luisa Banti,* Rome, pp. 223–239.

————. 1976. *Festòs e la civiltà minoica* I, Rome.

London, G. 1981. "Dung-Tempered Clay," *JFA* 8, pp. 189–195.

MacGillivray, J.A. 1984. "The Relative Chronology of Early Cycladic III," in MacGillivray and Barber, eds., 1984, pp. 70–77.

MacGillivray, J.A., and R.L.N. Barber, eds. 1984. *The Prehistoric Cyclades. Contributions to a Workshop on Cycladic Chronology,* Edinburgh.

Maniatis, Y., and M. Tite. 1975. "A Scanning Electron Microscope Examination of the Bloating of Fired Clays," *Transactions of the British Ceramic Society* 74, pp. 229–232.

————. 1978. "Ceramic Technology in the Aegean World during the Bronze Age," in *Thera and the Aegean World I. Papers Presented at the Second International Scientific Congress, Santorini, Greece, August 1978,* Ch. Doumas, ed., London, pp. 483–492.

————. 1981. "Technological Examination of Neolithic to Bronze Age Pottery from Central and South-East Europe," *Journal of Archaeological Science* 8, pp. 59–76.

Maniatis, Y., A. Simopoulos, and A. Kostikas. 1981. "Mössbauer Study of the Effect of Calcium Content on Iron Oxide Transformations in Fired Clays," *Journal of the American Ceramics Society* 64, pp. 263–269.

————. 1983. "Effect of Reducing Atmosphere on Minerals and Iron Oxides Developed in Fired Clays: The Role of Ca," *Journal of the American Ceramics Society* 66, pp. 773–781.

Manning, S.W. 1995. *The Absolute Chronology of the Aegean Early Bronze Age: Archaeology, Radiocarbon and History,* Sheffield.

Marinatos, S. 1929a. "Τὸ σπέος Εἰλειθυίας," *Praktika* 1929, pp. 95–104.

————. 1929b. "Πρωτομινωϊκὸς θολωτὸς τάφος παρὰ τὸ χωρίον Κράσι Πεδιάδος," *ArchDelt* 12 [1932], pp. 102–141.

————. 1930. "Ἀνασκαφαὶ ἐν Κρήτῃ," *Praktika* 1930 [1932], pp. 91–99.

————. 1932. "Archäologische Funde. Kreta," *AA* 1932, cols. 174–179.

————. 1933. "Funde und Forschungen auf Kreta," *AA* 1933, cols. 287–314.

Marthari, M. 1990. "Manufacture of the Local LBA Theran Pottery: Archaeological Consideration," in *Thera and the Aegean World III:* Volume One, *Archaeology. Proceedings of the Third International Congress, Santorini, Greece, 3–9 September 1989,* D.A. Hardy et al., eds., London, pp. 449–458.

Martlew, H. 1988. "Domestic Coarse Pottery in Bronze Age Crete," in French and Wardle, eds., 1988, pp. 421–424.

Mellaart, J. 1966. *The Chalcolithic and Early Bronze Ages in the Near East and Anatolia,* Beirut.

Mellink, M.J. 1956. "The Royal Tombs at Alaca Hüyük and the Aegean World," in *The Aegean and the Near East,* S.S. Weinberg, ed., Locust Valley, PA, pp. 39–58.

Michailidou, A. 2005. *Weight and Value in Pre-Coinage Societies: An Introduction* (*Meletemata* 42), Athens.

Moody, J. 1987. *The Environmental and Cultural Prehistory of the Khania Region,* Ph.D. diss., University of Minnesota.

Moody, J., O. Rackham, and G. Rapp. 1996. "Environmental Archaeology of Prehistoric NW Crete," *JFA* 23, pp. 273–297.

Morris, M.W. 2002. *Soil Science and Archaeology: Three Test Cases from Minoan Crete* (*Prehistory Monographs* 4), Philadelphia.

Mortzos, C.E. 1972. "Πάρτιρα: Μία πρώϊμος Μινωϊκή κεραμεική ὁμάς," Ἐπετηρίς Ἐπιστημονικῶν Ἐρευνῶν 3, pp. 386–419.

Mosso, A. 1910. *The Dawn of Mediterranean Civilisation,* London.

Muhly, J.D. 1996. "The First Use of Metals in the Aegean," in *The Copper Age in the Near East and Europe* (*Colloquium XIX: Metallurgy: Origins, Technology. XIIIth International Congress of Prehistoric and Protohistoric Sciences* 10), B. Bagolini and F. Lo Schiavo, eds., Forlì, pp. 75–84.

———. 2002. "Early Metallurgy in Greece and Cyprus," *Anatolian Metal* II (*Der Anschnitt. Zeitschrift für Kunst und Kultur im Bergbau Beiheft* 15), Ü. Yalçin, ed., Bochum, pp. 77–81.

———. 2004. "Chrysokamino and the Beginning of Metal Technology on Crete and in the Aegean," in *Crete Beyond the Palaces. Proceedings of the Crete 2000 Conference* (*Prehistory Monographs* 10), L.P. Day, M.S. Mook, and J.D. Muhly, eds., Philadelphia, pp. 283–289.

———. 2008. "Ayia Photia and the Cycladic Element in Early Minoan Metallurgy," in *Aegean Metallurgy in the Bronze Age. Proceedings of an International Symposium Held at the University of Crete, Rethymnon, Greece, on November 19–21, 2004,* I. Tzachili, ed., Athens, pp. 69–74.

Myer, G.H., and P.P. Betancourt. 1990. "The Fabrics at Kommos," in *Kommos* II: *The Final Neolithic through Middle Minoan III Pottery,* by P.P. Betancourt, Princeton, pp. 1–13.

Myer, G.H., K.G. McIntosh, and P.P. Betancourt. 1995. "Definition of Pottery Fabrics by Ceramic Petrography," in *Pseira* I: *The Minoan Buildings on the West Side of Area A* (*University Museum Monographs* 94), P.P. Betancourt and C. Davaras, eds., Philadelphia, pp. 143–153.

Mylonas, G.E. 1959. *Aghios Kosmas,* Princeton.

Nixon, L., J. Moody, and O. Rackham. 1988. "Archaeological Survey in Sphakia, Crete," *Echos du monde Classique/Classical Views* 7, pp. 159–173.

Noble, J.V. 1988. *The Techniques of Painted Attic Pottery,* New York.

Noll, W. 1978. "Material and Techniques of the Minoan Ceramics of Thera and Crete," in *Thera and the Aegean World I. Papers Presented at the Second International Scientific Congress, Santorini, Greece, August 1978,* Ch. Doumas, ed., London, pp. 492–505.

Noll, W., R. Holm, and L. Born. 1971–1974. "Chemie und Technik altkretischer Vasenmalerei vom Kamares-Typ, I–II," *Naturwissenschaften* 58, pp. 615–618.

Nowicki, K. 1999. "Final Neolithic Refugees or Early Bronze Age Newcomers? The Problem of Defensible Sites in Crete in the Late Fourth Millennium B.C.," in MELETEMATA: *Studies in Aegean Archaeology Presented to Malcolm H. Wiener as He Enters His 65th Year* (*Aegaeum* 20), P.P. Betancourt, V. Karageorghis, R. Laffineur, and W.-D. Niemeier, eds., Liège and Austin, pp. 575–581.

———. 2000. *Defensible Sites in Crete, c. 1200–800 B.C.* (*Aegaeum* 21), Liège.

———. 2002a. "A Middle Minoan II Deposit at the Refuge Site of Monastiraki Katalimata (East Crete)," *Aegean Archaeology* 5, pp. 27–45.

———. 2002b. "The End of the Neolithic in Crete," *Aegean Archaeology* 6, pp. 7–72.

———. 2004. "Report on Investigations in Greece. XI. Studies in 1995–2003," *Archeologia* [Warsaw] 55, pp. 75–100.

———. 2006. "New Evidence for the Final Neolithic in Crete," in *Πεπραγμένα Θ´ Διεθνούς Κρητολογικού Συνεδρίου* A (1), Herakleion, pp. 253–260.

———. 2008. *Monastiraki Katalimata: Excavation of a Cretan Refuge Site, 1993–2000* (*Prehistory Monographs* 24), Philadelphia.

Otto, B. 1985. *Die verzierte Keramik der Sesklo- und Diminikultur Thessaliens,* Mainz am Rhein.

Panagiotakis, N. 2004. "Contacts between Knossos and the Pediada Region in Central Crete," in *Knossos: Palace, City, State. Proceedings of the Conference in Herakleion Organized by the British School at Athens and the 23rd Ephoreia of Prehistoric and Classical Antiquities of Herakleion, in November 2000, for the Centenary of Sir Arthur Evans's Excavations at Knossos* (*BSA Studies* 12), G. Cadogan, E. Hatzaki, and A. Vasilakis, eds., London, pp. 177–186.

———. 2006. "Οικιστική τοπογραφία στην επαρχία Πεδιάδος από τη Νεολιθική περίοδο ως την Ύστερη Εποχή του Χαλκού," in *Πεπραγμένα Θ´ Διεθνούς Κρητολογικού Συνεδρίου* A (2), Herakleion, pp. 167–182.

Papadatos, Y. 2005. *Tholos Tomb Gamma: A Prepalatial Tholos Tomb at Phourni, Archanes* (*Prehistory Monographs* 17), Philadelphia.

———. 2007. "The Beginning of Metallurgy in Crete: New Evidence from the FN–EM I Settlement at Kephala-Petras, Siteia," in Day and Doonan, eds., 2007, pp. 154–167.

Paribeni, R. 1913. "Tomba di Siva," *Ausonia* 1913 (*Suppl.* 8), pp. 13–32.

Partridge, R. 1996. *Transport in Ancient Egypt,* London.

Pendlebury, H.W., J.D.S. Pendlebury, and M.B. Money-Coutts. 1937–1938a. "Excavations in the Plain of Lasithi. II," *BSA* 38, pp. 1–56.

Pernier, L. 1935. *Il palazzo minoico di Festòs* I, Rome.

Platon, N.E. 1950. "Χρονικά," *KrChron* 4, pp. 529–535.

————. 1974. "The Pre-Palace Minoan Period," in *History of the Hellenic World: Prehistory and Protohistory,* University Park, PA, pp. 116–130.

Provatakis, Th. 2007. *Λαϊκά επαγγέλματα και παραδοσιακή ζωή της Κρήτης,* Athens.

Psaropoulou, B. 1996. "Τα κεραμικά εργαστήρια των τελευταίων 100 χρόνων στην Κρήτη," in *Κεραμικά εργαστήρια στην Κρήτη από την αρχαιότητα ως σήμερα,* E. Gavrilaki, ed., Rethymnon, pp. 101–138.

Rambach, J. 2000. *Kykladen* II: *Die frühe Bronzezeit, frühbronzezeitliche Beigabensitten-Kreise auf den Kykladen. Relative Chronologie und Verbreitung,* Bonn.

Redding, R.W. 1989. *Decision Making in Subsistence Herding of Sheep and Goats in the Middle East,* Ph.D. diss., University of Michigan.

Relaki, M. 2004. "Constructing a *Region:* The Contested Landscapes of Prepalatial Mesara," in Barrett and Halstead, eds., 2004, pp. 170–188.

Renfrew, C. 1972. *The Emergence of Civilisation: The Cyclades and the Aegean in the Third Millennium B.C.,* London.

————. 1984. "From Pelos to Syros: Kapros Grave D and the Kampos Group," in MacGillivray and Barber, eds., 1984, pp. 41–54.

Renfrew, A.C., J.R. Cann, and J.E. Dixon. 1965. "Obsidian in the Aegean," *BSA* 60, pp. 225–247.

Sakellarakis, J. 1976. "Die Kykladen und Kreta," in *Kunst und Kultur der Kykladeninseln im 3. Jahrtausend v. Chr.,* J. Thimme, ed., Karlsruhe, pp. 149–158.

Sakellarakis, Y., and E. Sapouna-Sakellaraki. 1997. *Archanes: Minoan Crete in a New Light,* Athens.

Sampson, A. 1993. *Σκοτεινή Θαρρουνίων. Το σπήλαιο, ο οικισμός και το νεκροταφείο,* Athens.

————. 1997. *Το Σπήλαιο των Λιμνών στα Καστριά Καλαβρύτων. Μία προϊστορική θέση στην ορεινή Πελοπόννησο,* Athens.

————. 2002. *The Neolithic Settlement at Ftelia, Mykonos,* Rhodes.

————. 2006. *Η Προϊστορία του Αιγαίου. Παλαιολιθική—Μεσολιθική—Νεολιθική,* Athens.

Sbonias, K. 1999. "Social Development, Management of Production, and Symbolic Representation in Prepalatial Crete," in *From Minoan Farmers to Roman Traders:*

Sidelights on the Economy of Ancient Crete, A. Chaniotis, ed., Stuttgart, pp. 25–51.

Schlager, N. 2001a. "Pleistozäne, neolithische, bronzezeitliche und rezente Befunde und Ruinen im fernen Osten Kretas: Dokumentation 2000," *Jahreshefte des Österreichischen Archäologischen Instituts in Wien* 70, pp. 157–220.

———. 2001b. *Archaeological Survey in SE Crete: Site Documentation 2000 Report,* Vienna.

Schoep, I., and C. Knappett. 2004. "Dual Emergence: Evolving Heterarchy, Exploding Hierarchy," in Barrett and Halstead, eds., 2004, pp. 21–37.

Seager, R.B. 1912. *Explorations in the Island of Mochlos,* Boston and New York.

Shank, E. 2005. "New Evidence for Anatolian Relations with Crete in EM I–IIA," in EMPORIA: *Aegeans in the Central and Eastern Mediterranean* (*Aegaeum* 25), R. Laffineur and E. Greco, eds., Liège and Austin, pp. 103–106.

Shepard, A.O. 1956. *Ceramics for the Archaeologist,* Washington, D.C.

Sherratt, A.G. 1981. "Plow and Pastoralism: Aspects of the Secondary Products Revolution," in *Pattern of the Past: Studies in Honour of David Clarke,* I. Hodder, G. Isaac, and N. Hammond, eds., Cambridge, UK, pp. 261–305.

———. 1983. "The Secondary Exploitation of Animals in the Old World," *World Archaeology* 15, pp. 90–104.

Sklavenitis, Ch. 1996. "Κεραμικά κέντρα και λαϊκοί αγγειοπλάστες της Δυτικής Κρήτης," in *Κεραμικά εργαστήρια στην Κρήτη από την αρχαιότητά ως σήμερα,* E. Gavrilaki, ed., Rethymnon, pp. 79–100.

Soles, J.S. 1988. "Social Ranking in Prepalatial Cemeteries," in French and Wardle, eds., 1988, pp. 49–61.

Sperling, J.W. 1976. "Kum Tepe in the Troad: Trial Excavation, 1934," *Hesperia* 45, pp. 305–364.

Stos-Gale, Z.A. 1993. "The Origin of Metal Used for Making Weapons in Early and Middle Minoan Crete," in *Trade and Exchange in Prehistoric Europe. Proceedings of a Conference Held at the University of Bristol, April 1992,* C. Scarre and F. Healy, eds., Oxford, pp. 115–129.

———. 1998. "The Role of Kythnos and Other Cycladic Islands in the Origins of Early Minoan Metallurgy," in *Kea-Kythnos: History and Archaeology. Proceedings of an International Symposium, Kea-Kythnos, 22–25 June 1994* (Meletemata 27), L.G. Mendoni and A. Mazarakis Ainian, eds., Athens, pp. 717–736.

Thiébault, S. 2003. "Les paysages végétaux de Chypre au Néolithique: Premières données anthracologiques," in *Le Néolithique de Chypre. Actes du Colloque International organize par le department de Antiquité de Chypre et l'École Française d'Athènes, Nicosie 17–19 mai 2001* (*BCH Suppl.* 43), pp. 221–230.

Tite, M., and Y. Maniatis. 1975. "Scanning Electron Microscopy of Fired Calcareous Clays," *Transactions of the British Ceramic Society* 74, pp. 19–22.

Todaro, S. 2001. "Nuove prospettive sulla produzione in stile Pyrgos nella Creta meridionale: Il caso della pisside e della coppa su base ad anello," *Creta Antica* 2, pp. 11–28.

Tomkins, P. 2004. "Filling in the 'Neolithic Background,'" in Barrett and Halstead, eds., 2004, pp. 38–63.

Tomlinson, R. 1995. "Archaeology in Greece 1994–95," *AR* 41, pp. 1–74.

Tselios, T. 2008. "Pre-Palatial Copper Metalworking in the Mesara Plain, Crete," in *Aegean Metallurgy in the Bronze Age. Proceedings of an International Symposium Held at the University of Crete, Rethymnon, Greece, on November 19–21, 2004,* I. Tzachili, ed., Athens, pp. 123–139.

Tzedakis, I.G. 1966. " Ἀρχαιότητες καὶ μνημεῖα Δυτικῆς Κρήτης," *ArchDelt* 21 (Β΄, 2 Chronika), pp. 425–429.

———. 1967. " Ἀρχαιότητες καὶ μνημεῖα Δυτικῆς Κρήτης," *ArchDelt* 22 (Β΄, 2 Chronika), pp. 495–529.

———. 1968. " Ἀρχαιότητες καὶ μνημεῖα Δυτικῆς Κρήτης," *ArchDelt* 23 (Β΄, 2 Chronika), pp. 413–420.

———. 1984. "Le passage au Minoen ancien en Crète occidentale," in *Aux origines de l'hellénisme: la Crète et la Grèce: Hommage à Henri van Effenterre* (*Publications de la Sorbonne, Histoire ancienne et médiévale* 15), Paris, pp. 3–7.

Vagnetti, L. 1972–1973. "L'insediamento neolitico di Festòs," *ASAtene,* n.s. 34–35 [1975], pp. 7–138.

———. 1973. "Traces di due insediamenti neolitici nel territorio dell'antica Gortina," in *Antichità Cretesi. Studi in onore di Doro Levi,* G.P. Carratelli and G. Rizza, eds., Catania, pp. 1–9.

———. 1996. "The Final Neolithic: Crete Enters the Wider World," *Cretan Studies* 5, pp. 29–39.

Vagnetti, L., and P. Belli. 1978. "Characters and Problems of the Final Neolithic in Crete," *SMEA* 19, pp. 125–163.

Vagnetti, L., A. Christopoulou, and I. Tzedakis. 1989. "Saggi negli strati neolitici," in *Scavi a Nerokourou, Kydonias* (*Incunabula Graeca* 91: *Ricerche greco-italiane in Creta occidentale* 1), Rome.

Vallianos, Ch., and M. Padouva. 1986. *Τα κρητικά αγγεία του 19ου και 20ου αιώνα,* Voroi.

van Andel, T.H., and C.N. Runnels. 1995. "The Earliest Farmers in Europe," *Antiquity* 69, pp. 481–500.

van Effenterre, H., and M. van Effenterre. 1969. *Fouilles exécutées à Mallia. Le centre politique I. L'agora (1960–1966)* (*ÉtCrét* 17), Paris.

Vasilakis, A.S. 1987. "Ανασκαίφή ηεολιθικού σπιτιού στους Καλούς Λιμένες της Νότιας Κρήτης," in *Ειλαπίνη. Τόμος τιμητικός για τον Καθηγητή Νικόλαο Πλάτωνα,* L. Kastrinaki, G. Orphanou, and N. Giannadakis, eds., Herakleion, pp. 45–53.

————. 1989–1990. "Προϊστορικές θέσεις στη Μονή Οδηγήτριας, Καλοί Λιμένες," *Kretiki Estia* 3, pp. 11–80.

————. 1996. *Ο χρυσός και ο άργυρος στην Κρήτη κατά την πρώιμη περίοδο του χαλκού,* Herakleion.

————. 2008. "Silver Metalworking in Prehistoric Crete. An Historical Survey," in *Aegean Metallurgy in the Bronze Age. Proceedings of an International Symposium Held at the University of Crete, Rethymnon, Greece, on November 19–21, 2004,* I. Tzachili, ed., Athens, pp. 75–85.

Vaughan, S.J. 1990. "Petrographic Analysis of the Early Cycladic Wares from Akrotiri on Thera," in *Thera and the Aegean World III:* Volume I: *Archaeology. Proceedings of the Third International Congress, Santorini, Greece, 3–9 September 1989,* D.A. Hardy, et al., eds., London, pp. 470–487.

————. 2002. "Petrographic Analysis of Fabrics from the Pseira Cemetery," in *Pseira* VI: *The Pseira Cemetery* 1. *The Surface Survey* (*Prehistory Monographs* 5), P.P. Betancourt and C. Davaras, eds., Philadelphia, pp. 147–165.

Vaughan, S.J., G.H. Myer, and P.P. Betancourt. 1995. "Discussion and Interpretation of the Petrographic Data," in *Lerna: A Preclassical Site in the Argolid* III. *The Pottery of Lerna IV,* by J.B. Rutter, Princeton, pp. 693–710.

Voyatzoglou, M. 1972. *Τὰ πιθάρια στὸ Θραψανὸ τῆς Κρήτης,* Thessaloniki.

————. 1974. "The Jar Makers of Thrapsano in Crete," *Expedition* 16 (2), pp. 18–24.

————. 1984. "Thrapsano, Village of Jar Makers," in *East Cretan White-on-Dark Ware: Studies on a Handmade Pottery of the Early to Middle Minoan Periods* (*University Museum Monograph* 51), by P.P. Betancourt, Philadelphia, pp. 130–142.

Warren, P.M. 1972. *Myrtos: An Early Bronze Age Settlement in Crete* (*BSA Suppl.* 7), Oxford.

————. 1973. "Crete, 3000–1400 B.C.: Immigration and the Archaeological Evidence," in *Bronze Age Migrations in the Aegean: Archaeological and Linguistic Problems in Greek Prehistory,* R.A. Crossland and A. Birchall, eds., London, pp. 41–50.

————. 1984. "Early Minoan-Early Cycladic Chronological Correlations," in MacGillivray and Barber, eds., 1984, pp. 55–62.

————. 2004. "Part II. The Contents of the Tombs," in Alexiou and Warren, 2004, pp. 25–198.

Warren, P., and V. Hankey. 1989. *Aegean Bronze Age Chronology,* Bristol.

Warren, P., and J. Tzedhakis. 1974. "Debla, an Early Minoan Settlement in Western Crete," *BSA* 69, pp. 299–342.

Watrous, L.V., H. Blitzer, D. Haggis, and E. Zangger. 2000. "Economy and Society in the Gournia Region of Crete: A Preliminary Report on the 1992–1994 Field Seasons of the Gournia Project," in *Πεπραγμένα Η΄ Διεθνούς Κρητολογικού Συνεδρίου* A (3), Herakleion, pp. 471–483.

Watrous, L.V., and D. Hadzi-Vallianou. 2004. "Initial Growth in Social Complexity (Late Neolithic–Early Minoan I)" and "Register of Archaeological Sites," in *The Plain of Phaistos: Cycles of Social Complexity in the Mesara Region of Crete* (*Monumenta Archaeologica* 23), L.V. Watrous, D. Vallianou, and H. Blitzer, eds., Los Angeles, pp. 221–231, 525–540.

Weinberg, S. 1965. "The Aegean in the Stone and Early Bronze Age," in *Chronologies in Old World Archaeology,* R.W. Ehrich, ed., Chicago and London, pp. 285–320.

———. 1976. "The Cyclades and Mainland Greece," in *Kunst und Kultur der Kykladeninseln im 3. Jahrtausend v. Chr.,* J. Thimme, ed., Karlsruhe, pp. 142–144.

Whitelaw, T. 1983. "The Settlement at Fournou Korifi, Myrtos and Aspects of Early Minoan Social Organization," in Krzyszkowska and Nixon, eds., 1983, pp. 323–345.

Whitelaw, T., P.M. Day, E. Kiriatzi, V. Kilikoglou, and D.E. Wilson. 1997. "Ceramic Traditions at EM IIB Myrtos, Fournou Korifi," in *Texnh: Craftsmen, Craftswomen and Craftsmanship in the Aegean Bronze Age* (*Aegaeum* 16), R. Laffineur and P.P. Betancourt, eds., Liège and Austin, pp. 265–274.

Wilson, D.E. 1985. "The Pottery and Architecture of the Early Minoan IIA West Court House at Knossos," *BSA* 80, pp. 281–364.

———. 2007. "Early Prepalatial (EM I–EM II): EM I Well, West Court House, North-East Magazines and South Front Groups," in *Knossos Pottery Handbook: Neolithic and Bronze Age (Minoan)* (*BSA Studies* 14), N. Momigliano, ed., London, pp. 49–77.

Wilson, D.E., and P.M. Day. 1994. "Ceramic Regionalism in Prepalatial Central Crete: The Mesara Imports from EM I to EM IIA Knossos (with a Contribution by V. Kilikoglou)," *BSA* 89, pp. 1–87.

———. 2000. "EM I Chronology and Social Practice: Pottery from the Early Palace Tests at Knossos," *BSA* 95, pp. 21–62.

Wilson, D.E., P.M. Day, and N. Dimopoulou-Rethemiotaki. 2004. "The Pottery from Early Minoan I–IIB Knossos and Its Relations with the Harbour Site of Poros-Katsambas," in *Knossos: Palace, City, State. Proceedings of the Conference in Herakleion Organized by the British School at Athens and the 23rd Ephoreia of Prehistoric and Classical Antiquities of Herakleion, in November 2000, for the Centenary of Sir Arthur Evans's Excavations at Knossos* (*BSA Studies* 12), G. Cadogan, E. Hatzaki, and A. Vasilakis, eds., London, pp. 67–74.

———. 2008. "The Gateway Port of Poros-Katsambas: Trade and Exchange between North-Central Crete and the Cyclades in EB I–II," in Brodie et al., eds., 2008, pp. 261–270.

Wilson, D.E., and M. Eliot. 1984. "Ayia Irini, Period III: The Last Phase of Occupation at the E.B.A. Settlement," in MacGillivray and Barber, eds., 1984, pp. 70–77.

Xanthoudides, S. 1918a. "Μέγας πρωτομινωϊκὸς τάφος Πύργου," *ArchDelt* 4, pp. 136–170.

———. 1918b. "Πρωτομινωϊκοὶ τάφοι Μεσαρᾶς. Μαραθοκέφαλον," *ArchDelt* 4 (Parartema), pp. 15–22.

———. 1924. *The Vaulted Tombs of Mesara: An Account of Some Early Cemeteries of Southern Crete,* London.

———. 1927. "Some Minoan Potter's-Wheel Discs," in *Essays in Aegean Archaeology Presented to Sir Arthur Evans,* S. Casson, ed., Oxford, pp. 111–128.

Zervos, C. 1956. *L'art de la Crète néolithique et minoenne,* Paris.

Zois, A. 1968. "῎Ερευνα περὶ τῆς μινωϊκῆς κεραμεικῆς," *᾿Επετηρίς ᾿Επιστημονικῶν ᾿Ερευνῶν* 1, pp. 703–732.

Zschietzschmann, W. 1935. "Kykladenpfannen," *AA* 1935, cols. 652–668.

Index

burnishing, defined, 15, 56
butter, 40, 98

cakes, 97–98
calcite, 14, 16, 18, 20–21, 28–29
Calcite-Tempered Fabric Group, 28–29, 45, 65, 72, 74
calcium carbonate decomposition, 16, 21
calcium silicate formation temperature, 16, 21
carbon monoxide in firing pottery, 15
cattle, 9
ceramic petrography, 10, 20, 27–28
cerials. *See* grains
chaff, 14
chalices, 34–35, 56–58, 60–61, 74–75, 87, 103
    in burial ceremonies, 57, 61, 74
    with low base. *See* bowls, ring-footed
Chamaizi, 9
Chania, 2
cheese, 9, 40, 98–99
Chersonessos, 6
chert, 31
Chios, 76
chipped stone, 9
chlorite, 31
Chomatas, 52, 59
chronology, absolute, 7
Chrysokamino, 8, 9, 59, 100–103
Chryssi, 2
Classical Greek pottery, 48
clay platelets, microscopic, 15
clays, mixing, 20, 26–28
cloth, 9, 97, 110
coarse and fine fabrics, defined, 11
Coarse Dark Burnished Class, 44–47, 49, 64–65, 69–70
collared jars, 51, 82, 103
colonists, main discussion, 93–96
cooking dishes, 34, 36–37, 69–72, 87
cooking vessels, 19, 32, 69–72, 86–87
copper, 100–103
Cretan potters, modern, 20, 25–27

crinkled rim, 60
crucibles, 101–103
cups, 34–35, 44, 62, 66–67, 86–87
curds, 98
Cyclades, 7, 22, 28, 35, 38–39, 41, 60, 72–78, 82, 94–95, 102–103
Cycladic style vases, 72–78, 103
Cyprus, 98

Dark-on-Light Painted Ware, 47–48
Debla, 2, 6, 46, 64, 67, 69, 78
diabase, 31
Diaskari, 9
Dimeni Ware, 9, 21
dioritc, 30–31
Dodecanese, 94
donkey, 82, 97–99
Drakones, 5

Egypt, 53, 82, 98
Eileithyia Cave. *See* Amnissos
Ellenes, 2, 59
Embaros, 6
EM I form of wealth, new, defined, 99
Emporio, 45
epidote, 31
Episcopi, 2
Exo Potamoi, 6

fabric in pottery, defined, 10, 25
feeding bottle, 66
felt, 97
ferric oxide/ferrous oxide inversions, 15
Final Neolithic ceramic technology, main discussion, 13–16
Fine Dark Gray Burnished Class, 43, 56–64
Fine Gray Style, 7, 44, 72
Fine Gray Ware. *See* Fine Gray Style
flax, 97
fluxing agents, 16, 20–21
FN and EM I technology, mixed, 18–20
fortifications, 95, 103

fruit trees and fruits, 7, 10, 98
frying pans, 34, 37, 76–78, 103
Ftelia, 82

Gavdopoula, 2
Gavdos, 2, 64, 66–69
Gerani, 2, 98
Ghassulian culture, 83
Gieraki, 6
goats, 9–10, 95–96
goblets, 34–36, 44, 46–47, 87
Golan, 83
Gortyn, 5, 59
gourds, 39–41, 49–51, 54, 64, 86
Gournes, 2, 72, 101, 103
Gournia, 2, 8, 9, 52
grains, 7, 97
granodiorite, 30–31
grapes, 97
Greek mainland, 28
Grimani, 59
Grotta-Pelos Group, 7
ground stone tools, 9

Hagia Kyriaki, 5, 52, 55, 59, 109
Hagia Photia Sitias, 2, 5, 7, 9, 29, 44, 47,
    50, 52–53, 55, 57–59, 61–63, 66, 68,
    70–77, 88–90, 101–103
Hagia Triada, 2, 5, 52, 59
Hagio Gala, 76
Hagios Antonios, 8, 52
Hagios Charalambos, 2, 6, 47
Hagios Ioannis, 5, 52
Hagios Kyrillos, 2
Hagios Onouphrios, 5, 16–18, 49, 52, 54–
    55, 59
Hagios Onouphrios Style, 11, 16–18, 40,
    43, 47–53, 55–56, 88–90, 106–109
    Angular Red Inclusions, 49
    South Coast, 11, 49
Hagios Onouphrios Ware. See Hagios
    Onouphrios Style
Hagios Vasilios, 52

Halepa, 8
harbors, 8
harbor towns, 95
hercynite, 15
herringbone motif, 82–83
hides, 97
honey, 10, 40, 98
horns on vessels, 66–67, 69

Ierapetra, 2, 8–9
Ieropotamos River, 5
incense burner, 41, 75
Ioanimiti, 8
Israel, 4
itinerant potters, 26–27

jars, 34, 38–39, 44, 66, 68, 71, 86, 103
    with cut-outs, 34, 39, 41, 74–75
jugs, 16–17, 21, 38–40, 49–50, 55, 64–65,
    67, 70, 86–87, 103

Kalamafka, 6
Kalamaki, 5, 52
Kalathiana, 2
Kalavryta, 82
Kalivia, 5, 52
Kalo Chorio, 8, 47, 51–52, 57–59, 62, 79,
    100
Kaloi Limenes, 2, 5
Kamilari, 5
Kaminaki, 2, 6
Kampos Group, 7, 72, 75–77, 103
Kanli Kastelli. See Kyparissi
kaolinite, 26
Kastelli, 2
Kastri, 82
Kastria, 82
Katalimata, 8, 111
Katharo Plain, 6
Kato Metochi, 6
Katofigi, 6
Kavousi, 8, 9, 30, 52, 59, 100

Nea Roumata, 2, 66–68
Neapoli, 6
Neogene clays. *See* marl clays
Nerokourou, 97
Nisimos Plain, 6
nomenclature used in the text, 10–11

oats, 9
obsidian, 102
Odigitria, 5
olive oil, 9, 97–98, 106
olives, 9, 97–98, 100
Omalos Plain, 6
organic residue analysis, 69, 106
oxen, 82, 98–99

Pacheia Ammos, 8, 100
Pacheia Ammos Rock Shelter, 8, 13–14, 46
Palaikastro, 2, 9
Palestine, 4, 53
Panagia Paplinou Rousso Charakas, 8
Partira, 2, 59
Patrikies, 5, 52, 59
Pediada, 46
Pefka, 8
Pelos Style, 7, 75–76
Pephkos, 6
perfume, 97–98
Perivolia, 2
Petras, 9
Petrokephali, 5, 52
phacoids of marble, 28
Phaistos, 2, 5, 17, 52, 55, 59, 64, 94, 105, 110
phyllite, 18, 30–32
Phyllite-Tempered Fabric Group, 32, 45
pigs, 9
pit firing, defined, 15
pithari, 26
pithoi, 21–22, 29, 34, 40, 78–83, 103, 106–108
plagioclase, 30–31
Platanos, 2, 5

Plati, 6
Plattenkalk limestone, 28
Platyvola, 2, 52, 59, 64–65
Pobia, 5
Poliochni, 45, 53, 57
Poros Katsambas, 2, 5, 52, 59, 64, 72, 95, 100–103
Porti, 2
Priniatikos Pyrgos, 9
progressive changes with rising temperature, 15–16
Pseira, 2, 8, 9, 46–47, 52, 74
Psychro, 6
Pyrgos, 2, 5, 52, 58–60, 72–73
Pyrgos Style, 43–44, 56–64
pyroxene, 31
pyxides, 21, 34, 39–40, 43, 54–55, 62–63, 66, 68, 73–74, 78, 87, 103

quadruped-shaped vases, 50–51, 86
quartz, 30–32

radiocarbon dates, 7
Red to Brown Monochrome Class, 65–71, 106
reducing atmosphere, defined, 15
Rethymnon, 2
rock shelters, 13–14

Sahara Desert, 26
Salame Ware, 65
Saliagos, 82
Samos, 57
sandstone, 31
schist, 31–32
Scored Style, 43, 64–65
sea urchins, 40, 86
secondary products revolution, 9–10, 96–100
Selli, 5
Sendones, 5, 52, 59
Seriphos, 103
Sesklo Ware, 9, 21